Karl Marx and the Close of His System

A Criticism of the Marxist Theory of Value and the Price of Production

By Eugen von Böhm-Bawerk

PANTIANOS
CLASSICS

Published by Pantianos Classics

ISBN-13: 978-1-78987-145-6

First published in 1898

Contents

Introduction

As an author Karl Marx was enviably fortunate. No one will affirm that his work can be classed among the books which are easy to read or easy to understand. Most other books would have found their way to popularity hopelessly barred if they had laboured under an even lighter ballast of hard dialectic and wearisome mathematical deduction. But Marx, in spite of all this, has become the apostle of wide circles of readers, including many who are not as a rule given to the reading of difficult books. Moreover, the force and clearness of his reasoning were not such as to compel assent. On the contrary, men who are classed among the most earnest and most valued thinkers of our science, like Karl Knies, had contended from the first, by arguments that it was impossible to ignore, that the Marxian teaching was charged from top to bottom with every kind of contradiction both of logic and of fact. It could easily have happened, therefore, that Marx's work might have found no favour with any part of the public–not with the general public because it could not understand his difficult dialectic, and not with the specialists because they understood it and its weaknesses only too well. As a matter of fact. however, it has happened otherwise.

Nor has the fact that Marx's work remained a torso during the lifetime of its author been prejudicial to its influence. We are usually, and rightly, apt to mistrust such isolated first volumes of new systems. General principles can be very prettily put forward in the "General Sections" of a book, but whether they really possess the convincing power ascribed to them by their author, can only be ascertained when in the construction of the system they are brought face to face with all the facts in detail. And in the history of science it has not seldom happened that a promising and imposing first volume has never been followed by a second, just because, under the author's own more searching scrutiny, the new principles had not been able to stand the test of concrete facts. But the work of Karl Marx has not suffered in this way. The great mass of his followers, on the strength of his first volume, had unbounded faith in the yet unwritten volumes.

This faith was, moreover, in one case put to an unusually severe test. Marx had taught in his first volume [1] that the whole value of commodities was based on the labour embodied in them, and that by virtue of this "law of value" they must exchange in proportion to the quantity of labour which they contain; that, further, the profit or surplus value falling to the capitalist was the fruit of extortion practised on the worker; that, nevertheless, the amount of surplus value was not in proportion to the whole amount of the capital employed by the capitalist, but only to the amount of the "variable" part–that is, to that part of capital paid in wages–while the "constant capital," the capi-

iv

tal employed in the purchase of the means of production, added no surplus value. In daily life, however, the profit of capital is in proportion to the total capital invested; and, largely on this account, the commodities do not as a fact exchange in proportion to the amount of work incorporated in them. Here, therefore, there was a contradiction between System and fact which hardly seemed to admit of a satisfactory explanation. Nor did the obvious contradiction escape Marx himself. He says with reference to it, "This law" (the law, namely, that surplus value is in proportion only to the variable part of the capital), "clearly contradicts all *prima facie* experience." [2] But at the same time he declares the contradiction to be only a seeming one, the solution of which requires many missing links, and will be postponed to later volumes of his work. [3] Expert criticism thought it might venture to prophesy with certainty that Marx would never redeem this promise, because, as it sought elaborately to prove, the contradiction was insoluble. Its reasoning, however, made no impression at all on the mass of Marx's followers. His simple promise outweighed all logical refutations.

The suspense grew more trying when it was seen that in the second volume of Marx's work, which appeared after the master's death, no attempt had been made towards the announced solution (which, according to the plan of the whole work, was reserved for the third volume), nor even was the slightest intimation given of the direction in which Marx proposed to seek for the solution. But the preface of the editor, Friedrich Engels, not only contained the reiterated positive assertion that the solution was given in the manuscript left by Marx, but contained also an open challenge, directed chiefly to the followers of Rodbertus, that, in the interval before the appearance of the third volume, they should from their own resources attempt to solve the problem " how, not only without contradicting the law of value but even by virtue of it, an equal average rate of profit can and must be created."

I consider it one of the most striking tributes which could have been paid to Marx as a thinker that this challenge was taken up by so many persons, and in circles so much wider than the one to which it was chiefly directed. Not only followers of Rodbertus, but men from Marx's own camp, and even economists who did not give their adherence to either of these heads of the socialist school, but who would probably have been called by Marx "vulgar economists," vied with each other in the attempt to penetrate into the probable nexus of Marx's lines of thought, which were still shrouded in mystery. There grew up between 1885, the year when the second volume of Marx's *Capital* appeared, and 1894 when the third volume came out, a regular prize essay competition on the "average rate of profit," and its relation to the "law of value." [4] According to the view of Friedrich Engels–now, like Marx, no longer living–as stated in his criticism of these prize essays in the preface to the third volume, no one succeeded in carrying off the prize.

Now at last, however, with the long-delayed appearance of the conclusion of Marx's system, the subject has reached a stage when a definite decision is possible. For of the mere promise one could think as much red. Promises on the one side and arguments on the other were, in a sense, incommensurable. Even successful refutations of attempted solutions by others, though these attempts were held by their authors to have been conceived and carried out in the spirit of the Marxian theory, did not need to be acknowledged by the adherents of Marx, for they could always appeal from the faulty likeness to the promised original. But now at last this latter has come to light, and has procured for the thirty years' struggle a firm, narrow, and clearly defined battle-ground within which both parties can take their stand in order and fight the matter out, instead of on the one side contenting themselves with the hope of future revelations, or on the other passing, Proteus-like, from one shifting, unauthentic interpretation to another.

Has Marx himself solved his own problem? Has his completed system remained true to itself and to facts, Or not? To inquire into this question is the task of the following pages.

[1] English translation by Moore and Aveling, 1886; 2nd edition, 1888. (Sonnenschein.)

[2] *Das Kapital,* i., 1st edition, p. 285; 2nd edition, p.312.

[3] *Das Kapital,* i., 1st edition, pp. 285, 286, and 508 foot; 2nd edition, pp. 312 and 542 foot.

[4] From an enumeration of Loria's, I draw up the following list *(L'opera postuma di Carlo Marx; Nuevo Antologia,* vol. i., February, 1895, p. 18), which contains some essays not known to me; Lexis, *Jabrducher fur Nationalokonomie,* 1885, new series, vol. xi. pp. 452-65; Schmidt, *Die Durchschmittsprofitrate auf Grund des Marxschen Wertgesetzes,* Stuttgart, 1889; a discussion of the latter work by myself in the *Tubinger Zeitscbrift f. d. ges. Staatsw.,* 1890, p. 590 seq.; by Loria in the *Jahrbucher fur Nationalokonomie,* new series, vol. xx. (1890) pp. 272. seq.; Stiebling, *Das Wertgesetz und die Profitrate,* New York, 1890; Wolf, *Das Ratsel der Durchschnittsprofitrate bei Marx, Jahrb. f. Nationalok.,* third series, vol. ii. (1891), pp. 3521 seq; Schmidt again, *Neue Zeit,* 1892-3, Nos. 4 and 5; Lande, in the same, Nos. 19 and 20; Fireman, *Kritik der Marxschen Werttheorie, Jahrb. f. Nationalok.,* third series, vol. iii. (1892) pp. 793 seq.; finally Lafargue, Soldi, Coletti, and Graziadei in the *Critica Sociale* from July to November, 1894.

Chapter One - The Theory of Value and Surplus Value

THE pillars of the system of Marx are his conception of value and his law of value. Without them, as Marx repeatedly asserts, all scientific knowledge of economic facts would be impossible. The mode in which he arrives at his views with reference to both has been described and discussed times without number. For the sake of connection I must recapitulate briefly the most essential points of his argument.

The field of research which Marx undertakes to explore in order " to come upon the track of value" (i. 23) [1] he limits from the beginning to *commodities,* by which, according to him, we are not to understand all economic goods, but only those *products of labour* which are made for the market. [2] He begins with the "Analysis of a Commodity" (i.9). A commodity is, on one side, a useful thing, which by its properties satisfies human wants of some kind; and on the other, it forms the material medium of exchange value. He then passes to an analysis of this latter. "Exchange value presents itself in the first instance as the quantitative relation, the proportion, in which values in use of one kind are exchanged for values in use of another kind, a relation which constantly changes with time and place." Exchange value, therefore, appears to be something accidental. And yet there must be in this changing relation something that is stable and unchanging, and this Marx undertakes to bring to light. He does it in his well-known dialectical manner. "Let us take two commodities, wheat and iron, for example. Whatever may be their relative rate of exchange it may always be represented by an equation in which a given quantity of wheat is equal to a given quantity of iron: for example, 1 quarter wheat = 1 cwt. iron. What does this equation tell us? It tells us that there exists a common factor of the same magnitude in two different things, in a quarter of wheat and in a cwt. of iron. The two things are therefore equal to a third which is in itself neither the one nor the other. Each of the two, so far as it is an exchange value, must therefore be reducible to that third."

"This common factor," Marx goes on, "cannot be a geometrical, physical, chemical or other natural property of the commodities. Their physical properties come into consideration for the most part only in so far as they make the commodities useful, and so make them values in use. But, on the other hand, the exchange relation of commodities is obviously determined without reference to their value in use. Within this relation one value in use is worth just as much as any other, if only it is present in proper proportion. Or, as old Barbon says, "One sort of wares are as good as another, if the value be equal. There is no difference or distinction in things of equal value." As values in use commodities are above everything of different qualities; as exchange values they can only be of different quantities, and they can, therefore, contain no atom of value in use.

"If then we abstract from the value in use of commodities, there remains to them only one common property, that of being products of labour. But even as products of labour they have already, by the very process of abstraction, undergone a change under our hands. For if we abstract from the value in use of a commodity, we, at the same time, abstract from the material constituents and forms which give it a value in use. It is no longer a table, or a house, or yarn, or any other useful thing. All its physical qualities have disappeared. Nor is it any longer the product of the labour of the carpenter, or the mason, or the spinner, or of any other particular productive industry. With the useful character of the labour products there disappears the useful character of the labours embodied in them, and there vanish also the different concrete forms of these labours. They are no longer distinguished from each other, but are all reduced to identical human labour–abstract human labour.

"Let us examine now the residuum. There is nothing but this ghostly objectivity, the mere cellular tissue of undistinguishable human labour, that is, of the output of human labour without regard to the form of the output. All that these things have now to show for themselves is that human labour has been expended in their production–that human labour has been stored up in them; and as crystals of this common social substance they are–values."

With this, then, we have the conception of value discovered and determined. It is in dialectical form not identical with exchange value, but it stands, as I would now make plain, in the most intimate and inseparable relation to it. It is a kind of logical distillation from it. It is, to speak in Marx's own words, "the common element that manifests itself in the exchange relation, or exchange value, of commodities;" or again conversely, "the exchange value is the only form in which the value of commodities can manifest itself or be expressed " (i. 13).

After establishing the conception of value Marx proceeds to describe its measure and its amount. As labour is the substance of value so the amount of the value of all goods is measured by the quantity of labour contained in them, which is, in its turn, measured by its duration,–but not by that particular duration, or working time, which the individual who made the commodity has happened to need, but by the working time that is socially necessary. Marx defines this last as the "working time required to produce a value in use under the normal conditions of production, and with the degree of skill and intensity of labour prevalent in a given society" (i. 14). "It is only the quantity of socially necessary labour, or the working time socially necessary for the production of a value in use, which determines the amount of the value. The single commodity is here to be regarded as an average specimen of its class. Commodities, therefore, in which equal quantities of labour are embodied, or which can be produced in the same working time, have the same value. The value of one commodity is related to the value of any other commodity as the working time necessary for the production of the one is to that necessary for the production of the other. As values, all commodities are only specific quantities of crystallised working time." From all this is derived the subject-matter of the great "law of value," which is "immanent in the ex-change of commodities" (i. 141, 150), and governs exchange relations. It states, and must state, after what has gone before, that commodities are ex-changed in proportion to the socially necessary working time incorporated in them (i. 52). Other modes of expressing the same law are that "commodi-ties exchange according to their values" (see i. 142, 183; iii. 167), or that "equivalent exchanges with equivalent" (see i. 150, 183). It is true that in iso-lated cases according to momentary fluctuations of supply and demand pric-es occur which are over or under the values. But these "constant oscillations of market prices ... compensate and cancel each other, and reduce themselves to the average price as their inner law" (i. 151, note 37). In the long run "the socially necessary working time always asserts itself by main force, like an overruling natural law, in the accidental and ever fluctuating exchange rela-tions" (i. 52). Marx declares this law to be the "eternal law of the exchange of commodities" (i. 182), and "the rational element" and "the natural law of equilibrium" (iii. 167). The inevitably occurring cases already mentioned in which commodities are exchanged for prices which deviate from their values are to be looked upon, in regard to this rule, as "accidental" (i. 150, note 37), and he even calls the deviation "a breach of the law of the exchange of com-modities" (i. 142).

On these principles of the theory of value Marx founds the second part of the structure of his teaching, his renowned doctrine of surplus value. In this part he traces the source of the gain which capitalists obtain from their capi-tal. Capitalists lay down a certain sum of money, convert it into commodities, and then–with or without an intermediate process of production–convert these back again into more money. Whence comes this increment, this in-crease in the sum drawn out as compared with the sum originally advanced? or whence comes "the surplus value" as Marx calls it?[3]

Marx proceeds to mark off the conditions of the problem in his own peculi-ar way of dialectical exclusion. He first declares that the surplus value cannot originate either in the fact that the capitalist, as buyer, buys commodities regularly under their value, nor in the fact that the capitalist, as seller, sells them regularly over their value. So the problem presents itself in the follow-ing way: "The owner of money must buy the commodities at their value, then sell them at their value, and yet at the end of the process must draw out more money than he put in. Such are the conditions of the problem. *Hic Rhodus, hic salta!*" (i. 150 seq.)

The solution Marx finds in this, that there is one commodity whose value in use possesses the peculiar property of being a source of exchange value. This commodity is the capacity of labour, the working powers. It is offered for sale in the market under the twofold condition that the labourer is personally free, for otherwise it would not be his working powers only that would be for sale, but his whole person as a slave; and that the labourer is destitute of "all the means necessary for the realising of his working powers," for otherwise he would prefer to produce on his own account and to offer for sale his products rather than his working powers. It is by trading in this commodity that the capitalist obtains the surplus value; and he does so in the following way: The value of the commodity, "working powers," is regulated like any other commodity by the working time necessary for its reproduction; that is, in this case, by the working time which is needed to create so much means of subsistence as is required for the maintenance of the worker. If, for example, a working time of six hours is required in a given society for the production of the necessary means of subsistence for one day, and, at the same time, as we will suppose, this working time is embodied in three shillings of money, then the working powers of one day can be bought for three shillings. If the capitalist has concluded this purchase, the value in use of the working powers belongs to him and he realises it by causing the labourer to work for him. But if he made him work only so many hours a day as are embodied in the working powers themselves, and as must have been paid for in the buying of the same, no surplus value would arise. For, according to the assumption, six hours of labour could not put into the products in which they are embodied a greater value than three shillings, and so much the capitalist has paid as wages. But this is not the way in which capitalists act. Even if they have bought the working powers for a price which only corresponds to six hours' working time, they yet make the labourer work the whole day for them. And now in the product made during this day there are incorporated more hours of labour than the capitalist was obliged to pay for. He has, therefore, a greater value than the wages he has paid, and the difference is "surplus value," which falls to the capitalist.

Let us take an example: Suppose that a worker can spin ten pounds of cotton into yarn in six hours; and suppose this cotton has required twenty hours of labour for its own production and possesses accordingly a value of ten shillings; and suppose, further, that during the six hours of spinning the spinner uses up so much of his tools as corresponds to the labour of four hours and represents consequently a value of two shillings; then the total value of the means of production consumed in the spinning will amount to twelve shillings, corresponding to twenty-four hours' labour. In the spinning process the cotton "absorbs" another six hours of labour. Therefore the yarn that has been spun is, as a whole, the product of thirty hours of labour, and will have accordingly a value of fifteen shillings. On the supposition that the capitalist has made the hired labourer work only six hours in the day, the production of the yam has cost him at least fifteen shillings: ten shillings for cotton, two shillings for wear and tear of tools, three shillings for wages of labour. Here there is no surplus value.

It is quite a different thing, however, if the capitalist makes the labourer work twelve hours a day. In twelve hours the labourer works up twenty pounds of cotton in which forty hours of labour have been previously embodied, and which are, therefore, worth twenty shillings. He further uses up in tools the product of eight hours' labour, of the value of four shillings. But during a day he adds to the raw material twelve hours' labour, that is, a new value of six shillings. And now the balance-sheet stands as follows: The yarn produced during a day has cost in all sixty hours' labour, and has, therefore, a value of thirty shillings. The outlay of the capitalist amounted to twenty shillings for cotton, four shillings for wear and tear of tools, and three shillings for wages; in all, therefore, only twenty-seven shillings. There remains now a "surplus value" of three shillings.

Surplus value, therefore, according to Marx, is due to the fact that the capitalist makes the labourer work for him a part of the day without paying him for it. In the labourer's working-day two portions may be distinguished. In the first part–the "necessary working time"–the worker produces the means necessary for his own support, or the value of those means; and for this part of his labour he receives an equivalent in wages. During the second part-the "surplus working time"–he is worked for another's benefit *(exploité),* he produces "surplus value" without receiving any equivalent for it (i. 205 seq.). "All surplus value is in substance the embodiment of unpaid working time " (i. 554).

The following definitions of the amount of surplus value are very important and very characteristic of the Marxian system. The amount of surplus value may be brought into relation with various other amounts. The different proportions and proportionate numbers which arise out of this must be clearly distinguished.

First of all there are two elements to be distinguished in the capital which enables the capitalist to appropriate surplus values, each of which elements in relation to the origin of surplus value plays an entirely different part from the other. Really new surplus value can only be created by the living work which the capitalist gets the worker to perform. The value of the means of production which are used is maintained, and it reappears in a different form in the value of the product, but adds no surplus value. "That part of the capital, therefore, which is converted into the means of production, i.e., into raw material, auxiliary material, and implements of labour, does not alter the amount of its value in the process of production," for which reason Marx calls it "constant capital." "On the other hand, that part of capital which is converted into working powers does alter its value in the process of production. It reproduces its own equivalent and a surplus in addition," the surplus value. Therefore Marx calls it the "variable part of capital" or "variable capital" (i. 199) Now the proportion in which the surplus value stands to the advanced variable part of capital (in which alone the surplus value "makes good its value"), Marx calls the *rate of surplus value.* It is identical with the proportion in which the surplus working time stands to the necessary working time, or the unpaid labour to the paid, and serves Marx, therefore, as the exact expression for the extent to which labour is worked for another's benefit *(exploité)* (i. 207 seq.). If, for instance, the working time necessary for the worker to produce the value of his day's wages of three shillings amounts to six hours, while the actual number of hours he works in the day amounts to twelve, so that during the second six hours, which is surplus working time, he produces another value of three shillings, which is surplus value, then the surplus value is exactly equal to the amount of variable capital paid in wages, and the rate of the surplus value is reckoned at 100%.

Totally different from this is the rate of profit. The capitalist calculates the surplus value, which he appropriates, not only upon the variable capital but upon the total amount of capital employed. For instance, if the constant capital be £410, the variable capital £90, and the surplus value also £90, the rate of surplus value will be, as in the case just given, 100%, but the rate of profit only 18%, that is, £90 profit on an invested capital of £500.

It is evident, further, that one and the same rate of surplus value can and must present itself in very different rates of profit according to the composition of the capital concerned: the greater the variable and the less the constant capital employed (which latter does not contribute to the formation of surplus value, but increases the fund, in relation to which the surplus value, determined only by the variable part of capital, is reckoned as profit) the higher will be the rate of profit. For example, if (which is indeed almost a practical impossibility) the constant capital is nothing and the variable capital is £50, and the surplus value, on the assumption just made, amounts to 100%, the surplus value acquired amounts also to £50; and as this is reckoned on a total capital of only £50, the rate of profit would in this case also be quite 100%. If, on the other hand, the total capital is composed of constant and variable capital in the proportion of 4 to 1; or, in other words, if to a variable capital of £50 is added a constant capital of £200, the surplus value of £50, formed by the surplus value rate of 100%, has to be distributed on a capital of £250, and on this it represents only a profit rate of 20%. Finally, if the capital were composed in the proportions of 9 to 1, that is, £450 of constant to £50 of variable capital, a surplus value of £50 would fall on a total capital of £500, and the rate of profit would be only 10%.

Now this leads to an extremely interesting and important result, in pursuing which we are led to an entirely new stage of the Marxian system, the most important new feature which the third volume contains.

[1] I quote from the second edition (1872) of the first volume of *Das Kapital* from the 1885 edition of the second volume, and from the 1894 edition of the third volume; and unless I otherwise indicate, I always mean by iii. the first section of the third volume.
[2] I. 15, 17, 49, 87, and often. Compare also Adler, *Grundlagen der Karl Marxschen Kritik der bestehenden Volkswirtschaft,* Tubingen, 1887, pp. 210 and 213.
[3] I gave at the time in another place (Geschichte una Kritik der Kapitalzinstheorieen, 1884, pp. 421 seq.; English translation by Prof. Smart: Macmillan, 1890, pp. 367 seq.) an exhaustive account of this part of his doctrine. I make use of this account now, with numerous abridgments, such as the present purpose demands.

Chapter Two - The Theory of The Average Rate of Profit and the Price of Production

THAT result is as follows. The "organic composition" (iii. 124) of the capital is for technical reasons necessarily different in the different "spheres of production." In various industries which demand very different technical manipulations, the quantity of raw material worked up on one working day is very different; or, even, when the manipulations are the same and the quantity of raw material worked up is nearly equal, the value of that material may differ very much; as, for instance, in the case of copper and iron as raw materials of the metal industry; or finally the amount and value of the whole industrial apparatus, tools, and machinery, which are told off to each worker employed, may be different. All these elements of difference when they do not exactly balance each other, as they seldom do, create in the different branches of production a different proportion between the constant capital invested in the means of production and the variable capital expended in the purchase of labour. Every branch of economic production needs consequently a special, a peculiar, "organic composition" for the capital invested in it. According to the preceding argument, therefore, given an equal rate of surplus value, every branch of production must show a different, a special rate of profit, on the condition certainly, which Marx has hitherto always assumed, that commodities exchange with each other "according to their values," or in proportion to the work embodied in them.

And here Marx arrives at the famous rock of offence in his theory, so hard to steer past that it has formed the most important point of dispute in the Marxian literature of the last ten years. His theory demands that capitals of equal amount, but of dissimilar organic composition, should exhibit different profits. The real world, however, most plainly shows that it is governed by the law that capitals of equal amount, without regard to possible differences of organic composition, yield equal profits. We will let Marx explain this contradiction in his own words.

"We have thus shown that in different branches of industry varying rates of profit are obtained according to the differences in the organic composition of the capitals, and also, within given limits, according to their periods of turnover; and that, therefore, even with equal rates of surplus value, there is a law (or general tendency), *although only for capitals possessing the same organic composition,*–the same periods of turnover being assumed–that the profits are in proportion to the amounts of the capitals, and therefore equal amounts or capital yield in equal periods of time equal amounts of profit. The argument rests on the basis which has hitherto generally been the basis of our reasoning, *that commodities are sold according to their values.* On the other hand, there is no doubt that, in reality, not reckoning unessential, accidental, and self-compensating differences, the difference in the average rate of profit for different branches of industry *does not exist* and could not exist without upsetting the whole system of capitalist production. *It appears therefore that here the theory of value is irreconcilable with the actual movement of things,* irreconcilable with the actual phenomena of production, and that, on this account, the attempt to understand the latter must be given up." (iii. 131). How does Marx himself try to solve this contradiction?

To speak plainly his solution is obtained at the cost of the assumption from which Marx has hitherto started, viz., *that commodities exchange according to their values.* This assumption Marx now simply drops. Later on we shall form our critical judgment of the effect of this abandonment on the Marxian system. Meanwhile I resume my summary of the Marxian argument, and give one of the tabular examples which Marx brings forward in support of his view.

In this example he compares five different spheres of production, in each of which the capital employed is of different organic composition, and in making his comparison he keeps at first to the assumption which has been hitherto made, that commodities exchange according to their values. For the clear understanding of the following table, which gives the results of this assumption, it must be remarked that C denotes constant capital and V variable, and in order to do justice to the actual diversities of daily life, let us assume (with Marx) that the constant capitals employed are "worn out " in different lengths of time, so that only a portion, and that an unequal portion, of the constant capital in the different spheres of production, is used up in the year. Naturally only the used-up portion of constant capital–*the "used-up C"*–goes into the value of the product, whilst the whole *"employed C"* is taken into account in reckoning the rate of profit.

Capitals.	Surplus Value Rate.	Surplus Value.	Profit rate.	Used-up C.	Value of the Commodities
I. 80 C + 20 V	100%	20	20%	50	90
II. 70 C + 30 V	100%	30	30%	51	111
III. 60 C + 40 V	100%	40	40%	51	131
IV. 85 C + 15 V	100%	15	15%	5%	70
V. 95 C + 5 V	100%	5	5%	10	20

We see that this table shows in the different spheres of production where the exploitation of labour has been the same, very different rates of profit, corresponding to the different organic composition of the capitals. But we can also look at the same facts and data from another point of view. "The aggregate sum of the capital employed in the five spheres is = 500; the aggregate sum of the surplus value produced = 110; and the aggregate value of the commodities produced = 610. If we consider the 500 as a single capital of which I. to V. form only different parts (just as in a cotton manufactory in the different departments, in the carding-room, the roving-room, the spinning-room, and the weaving-room, a different proportion of variable and constant capital exists and the average proportion must be calculated for the whole manufactory), then in the first place the average composition of the capital of 500 would be 500 = 390 C + 110 V, or 78% C+ 22% V. Taking each of the capitals of 100 as being 1/5 of the aggregate capital its composition would be this average one of 78% C + 22% V; and likewise to every 100 would accrue as average surplus value 22%; therefore the average rate of profit would be 22%" (iii. '33-4). Now at what price must the separate commodities be sold in order that each of the five portions of capital should actually obtain this average rate of profit? The following table shows this. In it has been inserted the heading "Cost Price," by which Marx understands that part of the value of commodities which makes good to the capitalists the price of the consumed means of production and the price of the working power employed, but yet does not contain any surplus value or profit, so that its amount is equal to V + used-up C.

Capi-tals	Sur-plus Value	Used -up C	Value of the com-modities	Cost Price of the Commodi-ties	Price of the Commodi-ties	Prof-it rate	Devia-tion of the price from the value
I. 80 C + 20 V	20	50	90	70	92	22%	+ 2
II. 70 C + 30 V	30	51	111	81	103	22%	- 8
III. 60 C + 40 V	40	51	131	91	113	22%	- 18
IV. 85 C + 15 V	15	40	70	55	37	22%	+ 7
V. 95 C + 5 V	5	10	20	15	37	22%	+ 17

"Taken together," comments Marx on the results of this table, " the commodities are sold 2 + 7 + 17 = 26 over their value, and 8 + 18 under their value, so that the variations in price mutually cancel each other, either through an equal division of the surplus value or by cutting down the average profit of 22% on the invested capital to the respective cost prices of the commodities, I. to V.; in the same proportion *in which one part of the commodities is sold over its value another part will be sold under its value. And now their sale at such prices makes it possible that the rate of profit for I. to V. should be equal,* 22%, without regard to the different organic composition of the capital I. to V." (iii. 135).

Marx goes on to say that all this is not a mere hypothetical assumption, but absolute fact. The operating agent is competition. It is true that owing to the different organic composition of the capitals invested in various branches of production "the rates of profit which obtain in these different branches *are originally very different.*" But "these different rates of profit are reduced by competition to a common rate which is the average of all these different rates. The profit corresponding to this common rate, which falls to a given amount of capital, whatever its organic composition may be, is called *average profit.* That price of a commodity which is equal to its cost price plus its share of the yearly average profit of the capital employed (not merely that consumed) in its production (regard being had to the quickness or slowness of turnover) is its price of production" (iii. 136). This is in fact identical with Adam Smith's natural price, with Ricardo's price of production, and with the *prix necessaire* of the physiocrats (iii. 178). And the actual exchange relation of the separate commodities is *no longer determined by their values but by their prices of production;* or as Marx likes to put it "the values change into prices of production" (e.g., iii. 176). Value and price of production are only exceptionally and accidentally coincident, namely, in those commodities which are produced by the aid of a capital, the organic composition of which chances to coincide exactly with the average composition of the whole social capital. In all other cases value and production price necessarily and in principle part company. And his meaning is as follows. According to Marx we call "capitals which contain a greater percentage of constant, and therefore a smaller percentage of variable capital than the social average capital, capitals of *higher* composition; and contrariwise those capitals in which the constant capital fills a relatively smaller, and the variable a relatively larger space than in the social average capital are called capitals of *lower* composition." So in all those commodities which have been created by the aid of capital of "higher" composition than the average composition the price of production will be *above* their value, and in the it will be *under* the value. Or, opposite case commodities of the first kind will be necessarily and regularly sold over their value and commodities of the second kind under their value (iii. 142 seq., and often elsewhere).

The relation of the individual capitalists to the total surplus value created and appropriated in the whole society is finally illustrated in the following manner: "Although the capitalists of the different spheres of production in selling their commodities get back the value of the capital used up in the

16

production of these commodities, they do not thereby recover the *surplus value,* and therefore profit, created in their own particular spheres, by the production of these commodities, but only so much surplus value, and therefore profit, as falls by an equal division to every aliquot part of the whole capital, from the total surplus value or total profit which the entire capital of society has created in a given time, in all the spheres of production taken together. Every 100 of invested capital, whatever its composition, secures in every year, or other period of time, the profit which, for this period, falls due to a 100 as a given part of the total capital. So far as profit is concerned, the different capitalists are in the position of simple members of a joint stock company, in which the profits are divided into equal shares on every 100, and therefore for the different capitalists vary only according to the amount of capital invested by each in the common undertaking, according to the relative extent of his participation in the common business, according to the number of his shares" (iii. 136 seq.). Total profit and total surplus value are identical amounts (iii. 151, 152). And the average profit is nothing else "than the total amount of surplus value divided among the amounts of capital in every sphere of production in proportion to their quantities" (iii. 153).

An important consequence arising from this is that the profit which the individual capitalist draws is clearly shown not to arise only from the work performed by himself (iii. 149), but often proceeds for the most part, and sometimes entirely (for example, in the case of mercantile capital), from labourers with whom the capitalist concerned has no connection whatever. Marx, in conclusion, puts and answers one more question, which he regards as the specially difficult question, the question namely, In what manner "does this adjustment of profits to a common rate of profit take place, since it is evidently a result and not a starting point?"

He first of all puts forward the view that in a condition of society in which the capitalist system is not yet dominant, and in which, therefore, the labourers themselves are in possession of the necessary means of production, commodities are actually exchanged according to their real value, and the rates of profit could not therefore be equalised. But as the labourers could always obtain and keep for themselves an equal surplus value for an equal working time–i.e., an equal value over and above their necessary wants–the actually existing difference in the profit rate would be "a matter of indifference, just as to-day it is a matter of indifference to the hired labourer by what rate of profit the amount of surplus value squeezed out of him is represented" (iii. 155). Now as such conditions of life in which the means of production belong to the worker, are historically the earlier, and are found in the old as well as in the modern world, with peasant proprietors, for instance, and artisans, Marx thinks he is entitled to assert that it is "quite in accordance with facts to regard the values of commodities as, not only theoretically but also historically, prior to the prices of production" (iii. 156).

In societies organised on the capitalist system, however, this changing of values into prices of production and the equalisation of the rates of profit which follows, certainly do take place. There are some long preliminary discussions, in which Marx treats of the formation of market value and market price with special reference to the production of separate parts of commodities produced for sale under conditions of varying advantage. And then he expresses himself as follows very clearly and concisely on the motive forces of this process of equalisation and on its mode of action: "If commodities are ... sold according to their values ... very different rates of profit are obtained· · · · Capital withdraws itself, however, from a sphere with a low rate of profit, and throws itself into another which yields a higher profit. By this continual interchange, or, in a word, by its apportionment between the different spheres, as the rate of profit sinks here and rises there, such a relation of supply to demand is created as to make the average profit in the different spheres of production the same, and thus values are changed into prices of production" (iii. 175-6). [1]

[1] W. Sombart in the classical, clear, and comprehensive account of the concluding volume of the Marxian system which he lately gave in the *Archiv fur Sozile Gesetzgebung* (vol. vii., part 4, pp. 555 seq.), also regards the passages quoted in the text as those which contain the strict answer to the problem given (Ibid., p. 564). We shall by and by have to deal more at large with this important and ingenious, but critically, I think, unsatisfactory essay.

Chapter Three - The Question of the Contradiction

MANY years ago, long before the abovementioned prize essays on the compatibility of an equal average rate of profit with the Marxian law of value had appeared, the present writer had expressed his opinion on this subject in the following words: "Either products do actually exchange in the long run in proportion to the labour attaching to them–in which case an equalisation of the gains of capital is impossible; or there is an equalisation of the gains of capital–in which case it is impossible that products should continue to exchange in proportion to the labour attaching to them." [1]

From the Marxian camp the actual incompatibility of these two propositions was first acknowledged a few years ago by Conrad Schmidt. [2] Now we have the authoritative confirmation of the master himself. He has stated concisely and precisely that an equal rate of profit is only possible when the conditions of sale are such that some commodities are sold above their value, and others under their value, and thus are not exchanged in proportion to the labour embodied in them. And neither has he left us in doubt as to which of the two irreconcilable propositions conforms in his opinion to the actual facts. He teaches, with a clearness and directness which merit our gratitude, that it is the equalisation of the gains of capital. And he even goes so far as to say, with the same directness and clearness, that the several commodities do not actually exchange with each other in proportion to the labour they contain, but that they exchange in that varying proportion to the labour, which is rendered necessary by the equalisation of the gains of capital.

In what relation does this doctrine of the third volume stand to the celebrated law of value of the first volume? Does it contain the solution of the seeming contradiction looked for with so much anxiety? Does it prove "how not only without contradicting the law of value, but even by virtue of it, an equal average rate of profit can and must be created?" Does it not rather contain the exact opposite of such a proof, viz., the statement of an actual irreconcilable contradiction, and does it not prove that the equal average rate of profit can only manifest itself if, and because, the alleged law of value does not hold good?

I do not think that any one who examines the matter impartially and soberly can remain long in doubt. In the first volume it was maintained, with the greatest emphasis, that all value is based on labour and labour alone, and that values of commodities were in proportion to the working time necessary for their production. These propositions were deduced and distilled directly and exclusively from the exchange relations of commodities in which they were "immanent." We were directed "to start from the exchange value, and exchange relation of commodities, in order to come upon the track of the value concealed in them" (i. 23). The value was declared to be "the common factor which appears in the exchange relation of commodities" (i. 13). We were told, in the form and with the emphasis of a stringent syllogistic conclusion, allowing of no exception, that to set down two commodities as equivalents in exchange implied that "a common factor *of the same magnitude*" existed in both, to which each of the two *"must* be reducible" (i. 11). Apart, therefore, from temporary and occasional variations which "appear to be a breach of the law of the exchange of commodities" (i. 142), commodities which embody the same amount of labour *must* on principle, in the long run, exchange for each other. And now in the third volume we are told briefly and drily that what, according to the teaching of the first volume *must* be, is not and never can be; that individual commodities do and must exchange with each other in a proportion different from that of the labour incorporated in them, and this not accidentally and temporarily, but of necessity and permanently.

I cannot help myself; I see here no explanation and reconciliation of a contradiction, but the bare contradiction itself. Marx's third volume contradicts the first. The theory of the average rate of profit and of the prices of production cannot be reconciled with the theory of value. This is the impression which must, I believe, be received by every logical thinker. And it seems to have been very generally accepted. Loria, in his lively and picturesque style, states that he feels himself forced to the "harsh but just judgment" that Marx "instead of a solution has presented a mystification." He sees in the publication of the third volume " the Russian campaign" of the Marxian system, its "complete theoretic bankruptcy," a "scientific suicide," the "most explicit surrender of his own teaching" *(l'abdicazione piu esplicita alla dottrina stessa),* and the "full and complete adherence to the most orthodox doctrine of the hated economists." [3]

And even a man who is so close to the Marxian system as Werner Sombart, says that a "general head-shaking" best represents the probable effect produced on most readers by the third volume. "Most of them," he says, "will not be inclined to regard 'the solution' of 'the puzzle of the average rate of profit' as a 'solution'; they will think that the knot has been cut, and by no means untied. For, when suddenly out of the depths emerges a 'quite ordinary' theory of cost of production, it means that the celebrated doctrine of value has come to grief. For, if I have in the end to explain the profits by the cost of production, wherefore the whole cumbrous apparatus of the theories of value and surplus value?" [4] Sombart certainly reserves to himself another judgment. He attempts to save the theory in a way of his own, in which, however, so much of it is thrown overboard that it seems to me very doubtful if his efforts have earned the gratitude of any person concerned in the matter. I shall by and by more closely examine this at all events interesting and instructive attempt. But, before the posthumous apologist, we must give the master himself the careful and attentive hearing which so important a subject deserves.

Marx himself must, of course, have foreseen that his solution would incur the reproach of being no solution at all, but a surrender of his law of value. To this prevision is evidently due an anticipatory self-defence which, if not in form yet in point of fact, is found in the Marxian system; for Marx does not omit to interpolate in numerous places the express declaration that, in spite of exchange relations being directly governed by prices of production, which differ from the values, all is nevertheless moving within the lines of the law of value and this law, "in the last resort" at least, governs prices. He tries to make this view plausible by several inconsequent observations and explanations. On this subject he does not use his customary method of a formal close line of reasoning, but gives only a series of running, incidental remarks which contain different arguments, or turns of expression which may be interpreted as such. In this case it is impossible to judge on which of these arguments Marx himself intended to place the greatest weight, or what was his conception of the reciprocal relations of these dissimilar arguments. However that may be, we must, in justice to the master as well as to our own critical problem, give each of these arguments the closest attention and impartial consideration.

The running remarks appear to me to contain the following four arguments in favour of a partly or wholly permanent validity of the law of value.

First argument: Even if the *separate* commodities are being sold either above or below their values, these reciprocal fluctuations cancel each other, and in the community itself–taking into account all the branches of production–the *total of the prices of production* of the commodities produced still remains *equal to the sum of their values* (iii. 138).

Second argument: The law of value governs the *movement of prices,* since the diminution or increase of the requisite working time makes the prices of production rise or fall (iii. 158, 156).

Third argument: The law of value, Marx affirms, governs with undiminished authority the exchange of commodities in *certain "primary" stages,* in which the change of values into prices of production has not yet been accomplished.

Fourth argument: In a complicated economic system the law of value regulates the prices of production at least *indirectly and in the last resort,* since the total value of the commodities, determined by the law of value, determines the total surplus value. The latter, however, regulates the amount of the average profit, and therefore the general rate of profit (iii. 159). Let us test these arguments, each one on its own merits.

FIRST ARGUMENT

It is admitted by Marx that separate commodities exchange with each other either over or under their value according as the share of constant capital employed in their production is above or below the average. Stress is, however, laid on the fact that these individual deviations which take place in opposite directions compensate or cancel each other, so that the sum total of all prices paid corresponds exactly with the sum of all values. "In the same proportion in which one part of the commodities is sold above its value another part will be sold under its value" (iii. 135). "The aggregate price of the commodities I. to V. (in the table given by Marx as an example) would therefore be equal to their aggregate values, and would therefore be, in fact, a money expression of the aggregate amount of labour, both past and recent, contained in the commodities I. to V. And in this way in the community itself—when we regard the total of all the branches of production–the sum of the prices of production of the commodities manufactured is equal to the sum of their values" (iii. 138). From this, finally, the argument is more or less clearly deduced that at any rate for the sum of all commodities, or, for the community as a whole, the law of value maintains its validity. "Meanwhile it resolves itself into this—that by as much as there is too much surplus value in one commodity there is too little in another, and therefore the *deviations from value* which lurk in the prices of production *reciprocally cancel each other.* In capitalistic production as a whole *'the general law maintains itself as the governing tendency,'* only in a very complex and approximate manner, as the constantly changing average of perpetual fluctuations" (iii. 140).

This argument is not new in the Marxian literature. In similar circumstances it was maintained, a few years ago, by Conrad Schmidt, with great emphasis, and perhaps with even greater clearness of principle than now by Marx himself. In his attempt to solve the riddle of the average rate of profit Schmidt also, while he employed a different line of argument from Marx, arrived at the conclusion that separate commodities cannot exchange with each other in proportion to the labour attaching to them. He too was obliged to ask the question whether, in face of this fact, the validity of Marx's law of value could any longer be maintained, and he supported his affirmative opinion on the very argument that has just been given. [5]

I hold the argument to be absolutely untenable. I maintained this at the time against Conrad Schmidt, and I have no occasion to-day in relation to Marx himself to make any alteration in the reasoning on which I founded my opinion then. I may content myself now with simply repeating it word for word. In opposing Conrad Schmidt, I asked how much or how little of the celebrated law of value remained after so much had practically been given up, and then continued: "That not much remains will be best shown by the efforts which the author makes to prove that, in spite of everything, the law of value maintains its validity. After he has admitted that the actual prices of commodities differ from their values, he remarks that this divergence only relates to those prices obtained by *separate commodities,* and that it disappears as soon as one considers the sum of all separate commodities, the yearly national produce, and that the total price which is paid for the whole national produce taken together does certainly coincide entirely with the amount of value actually embodied in it (p. 51). I do not know whether I shall be able to show sufficiently the bearings of this statement, but I shall at least attempt to indicate them.

"What then, we ask, is the chief object of the 'law of value'? It is nothing else than the elucidation of the exchange relations of commodities as they actually appear to us. We wish to know, for instance, why a coat should be worth as much in exchange as twenty yards of linen, and ten pounds of tea as much as half a ton of iron, &c. It is plain that Marx himself so conceives the explanatory object of the law of value. There can clearly only be a question of an exchange *relation* between different separate commodities *among each other.* As soon, however, as one looks at all commodities *as a whole* and sums up the prices, one must studiously and of necessity avoid looking at the relations existing inside of this whole. The internal relative differences of price do compensate each other in the sum total. For instance, what the tea is worth more than the iron the iron is worth less than the tea and *vice versa.* In any case, when we ask for information regarding the exchange of commodities in political economy it is no answer to our question to be told the total price which they fetch when taken altogether, any more than if, on asking by how many fewer minutes the winner in a prize race had covered the course than his competitor, we were to be told that all the competitors together had taken twenty-five minutes and thirteen seconds.

"The state of the case is this: To the question of the problem of value the followers of Marx reply first with their law of value, i.e., that commodities exchange in proportion to the working time incorporated in them. Then they–covertly or openly–revoke this answer in its relation to the domain of the exchange of separate commodities, the one domain in which the problem has any meaning, and maintain it in full force only for the whole aggregate national produce, for a domain therefore in which the problem, being without object, could not have been put at all. As an answer to the strict question of the Problem of value the law of value is avowedly contradicted by the facts, and in the only application in which it is not contradicted by them it is no longer an answer to the question which demanded a solution, but could at best only be an answer to some other question.

"It is, however, not even an answer to another question; it is no answer at all; it is simple tautology. For, as every economist knows, commodities do eventually exchange with commodities–when one penetrates the disguises due to the use of money. Every commodity which comes into exchange is at one and the same time a commodity and the price of what is given in exchange for it. The aggregate of commodities therefore is identical with the aggregate of the prices paid for them; or, the price of the whole national produce is nothing else than the national produce itself. Under these circumstances, therefore, it is quite true that the total price paid for the entire national produce coincides exactly with the total amount of value or labour incorporated in it. But this tautological declaration denotes no increase of true knowledge, neither does it serve as a special test of the correctness of the alleged law that commodities exchange in proportion to the labour embodied in them. For in this manner one might as well, or rather as unjustly, verify any other law one pleased–the law, for instance, that commodities exchange according to the measure of their specific gravity. For if certainly as a 'separate ware' 1 lb. of gold does not exchange with 1 lb. of iron, but with 40,000 lbs. of iron; still, the *total price* paid for 1 lb. of gold and 40,000 lbs. of iron *taken together* is nothing more and nothing less than 40,000 lbs. of iron and 1 lb. of gold. The total weight, therefore, of the total price–40,001 lbs.–corresponds exactly to the like total weight of 40,001 lbs. incorporated in the whole of the commodities. Is weight consequently the true standard by which the exchange relation of commodities is determined?"

I have nothing to omit and nothing to add to this judgment in applying it now to Marx himself, except perhaps that in advancing the argument which has just been under criticism Marx is guilty of an additional error which cannot be charged against Schmidt. For, in the passage just quoted from page 140 of the third volume, Marx seeks, by a general dictum concerning the way in which the law of value operates, to gain approval for the idea that a certain real authority may still be ascribed to it, even if it does not rule in separate cases. After saying that the "deviations" from value, which are found in the prices of production, cancel each other, he adds the remark that "in capitalistic production as a whole the general law maintains itself as the governing tendency, for the most part only in a very complex and approximate manner as the constantly changing *average of perpetual fluctuations.*"

Here Marx confounds two very different things: *an average of fluctuations, and an average between permanently and fundamentally unequal quantities.* He is so far quite right, that many a general law holds good solely because an average resulting from constant fluctuations coincides with the rule declared by the law. Every economist knows such laws. Take, for example, the law that prices equal costs of production–that apart from special reasons for inequality there is a tendency for wages in different branches of industry, and for profits of capital in different branches of production, to come to a level, and every economist is inclined to acknowledge these laws as "laws," although perhaps there may be no absolutely exact agreement with them in any single case; and therefore even the power to refer to a mode of action operating on the whole, and on the average, has a strongly captivating influence.

But the case in favour of which Marx uses this captivating reference is of quite a different kind. In the case of prices of production which deviate from the "values," it is not a question of fluctuations, but of necessary and permanent divergences.

Two commodities, A and B, which contain the same amount of labour, but have been produced by capitals of different organic composition, do not fluctuate round the same average point, say, for example, the average of fifty shillings; but each of them assumes permanently a different level of price: for instance, the commodity A, in the production of which little constant capital, demanding but little interest, has been employed, the price level of forty shillings; and the commodity B, which has much constant capital to pay interest on, the price level of sixty shillings, allowance being made for fluctuation round each of these deviating levels. If we had only to deal with fluctuations round one and the same level, so that the commodity A might stand at one moment at forty-eight shillings and the commodity B at fifty-two shillings, and at another moment the case were reversed, and the commodity A stood at fifty-two shillings and the commodity B only reached forty-eight, then we might indeed say that in the average the price of both of these commodities was the same, and in such a state of things, if it were seen to obtain universally, one might find, in spite of the fluctuations, a verification of the "law" that commodities embodying the same amount of labour exchange on an equal footing.

When, however, of two commodities in which the same amount of labour is incorporated, one permanently and regularly maintains a price of forty shillings and the other as permanently and regularly the price of sixty shillings, a mathematician may indeed strike an average of fifty shillings between the two; but such an average has an entirely different meaning, or, to be more accurate, has no meaning at all with regard to our law. A mathematical average may always be struck between the most unequal quantities, and when it has once been struck the deviations from it on either side always "mutually cancel each other" according to their amount; by the same amount exactly by which the one exceeds the average the other must of necessity fall short. But it is evident that necessary and permanent differences of prices in commodities of the same cost in labour, but of unequal composition as regards capital, cannot by such playing with "average" and "deviations that cancel each other" be turned into a confirmation of the alleged law of value instead of a refutation.

We might just as well try in this way to prove the proposition that animals of all kinds, elephants and May-flies included, have the same length of life; for while it is true that elephants live on an average one hundred years and May-flies only a single day, yet between these two quantities we can strike an average of fifty years. By as much time as the elephants live longer than the flies, the flies live shorter than the elephants. The deviations from this average "mutually cancel each other," and consequently on the whole and on the average the law that all kinds of animals have the same length of life is established!

Let us proceed.

SECOND ARGUMENT

In various parts of the third volume Marx claims for the law of value that it "governs the movement of prices," and he considers that this is proved by the fact that where the working time necessary for the production of the commodities decreases, there also prices fall; and that where it increases prices also rise, other circumstances remaining equal. [6]

This conclusion also rests on an error of logic so obvious that one wonders Marx did not perceive it himself. That in the case of "other circumstances remaining equal" prices rise and fall according to the amount of labour expended proves clearly neither more nor less than that labour is one factor in determining prices. It proves, therefore, a fact upon which all the world is agreed, an opinion not peculiar to Marx, but one acknowledged and taught by the classical and "vulgar economists." But by his law of value Marx had asserted much more. He had asserted that, barring occasional and momentary fluctuations of demand and supply, the labour expended was the sole factor which governed the exchange relations of commodities. Evidently it could only be maintained that *this* law governs the movement of prices if a permanent alteration in prices could not be produced or promoted by any other cause than the alteration in the amount of working time. This, however, Marx does not and cannot maintain; for it is among the results of his own teaching that an alteration in prices must occur when, for instance, the expenditure of labour remains the same, but when, owing to such circumstances as the shortening of the processes of production, the organic composition of the capital is changed. By the side of this proposition of Marx we might with equal justification place the other proposition, that prices rise or fall when, other conditions remaining equal, the length of time during which the capital is invested increases or decreases. If it is impossible to prove by the latter proposition that the length of time during which the capital is invested is the sole factor that governs exchange relations, it is equally impossible to regard the fact that alterations in the amounts of the labour expended affect the movements of prices, as a confirmation of the alleged law that labour alone governs the exchange relations.

THIRD ARGUMENT

This argument has not been developed with precision and clearness by Marx, but the substance of it has been woven into those processes of reasoning, the object of which was the elucidation of the "truly difficult question" "how the adjustment of the profits to the general rate of profit takes place" (iii. 153 seq.).

The kernel of the argument is most easily extracted in the following way. Marx affirms, and must affirm, that "the rates of profits are originally very different" (iii. 136), and that their adjustment to a general rate of profits is primarily "a result, and cannot be a starting, point " (iii. 153). This thesis further contains the claim that there exist certain "primitive" conditions in which the change of values into prices of production which leads to the adjustment of the rates of profit, has not yet taken place, and which therefore are still under the complete and literal dominion of the law of value. A certain region is consequently claimed for this law in which its authority is perfectly absolute.

Let us inquire more closely what this region is, and see what arguments Marx adduces to prove that the exchange relations in it are actually determined by the labour incorporated in the commodities.

According to Marx the adjustment of the rate of profit is dependent on two assumptions. Firstly, on a capitalistic system of production being in operation (iii. 154); and secondly, on the levelling influence of *competition* being in effective action (iii. 136, 151, 159, 175, 176). We must, therefore, logically look for the "primitive conditions" under which the pure regime of the law of value prevails where one or other of these assumed conditions does not exist (or, of course, where both are absent).

On the first of these cases Marx has himself spoken very fully. By a very detailed account of the processes which obtain in a condition of society where capitalistic production does not yet prevail, but "where the means of production belong to the worker," he shows the prices of commodities in this stage to be exclusively determined by their values. In order to enable the reader to judge impartially how far this account is really convincing, I must give the full text of it:–

"The salient point will be best shown in the following way. Suppose the workers themselves to possess each his own means of production, and to exchange their commodities with each other. These commodities would not then be the product of capital. The value of the tools and raw material employed in the different branches of labour would be different according to the special nature of the work, and also, apart from inequality of value in the means of production employed, different amounts of these means would be required for given amounts of labour, according as one commodity could be finished in an hour and another only in a day, &c. Let us suppose, further, that these labourers work the same time, on an average, allowing for the adjustments which result from differences of intensity, &c., in work. Of any two workers, then, both would, firstly, in the commodities which represent the produce of their day's labour, have replaced their outlays, that is, the cost prices of the consumed means of production. These would differ according to the technical nature of their branches of industry. Secondly, both would have created the same amount of new value, i.e., the value of the day's labour added to the means of production. This would contain their wages plus the surplus value, the surplus work above their necessary wants, of which the result, however, would belong to themselves. *If we express ourselves in capitalistic terms, both receive the same wages plus the same profit,* but also the value, represented, for instance, by the produce of a working day of ten hours. But in the first place the values of their commodities would be different. In commodity I., for example, there would be a larger share of value for the expended means of production than in commodity II. The rates of profit also would be very different for I. and II., if we here consider as rates of profit the proportion of the surplus value to the total value of the employed means of production. The means of subsistence which I. and II. consume daily during the process of production, and which represent the wages of labour, form here that part of the advanced means of production which we usually call variable capital. But the *surplus value would be, for the same working time,* the same for I. and II.; or, to go more closely into the matter, as I. and II., each, receive the value of the produce of one day's work, they receive, after deducting the value of the advanced "constant" elements, equal values, one part of which may be looked upon as compensation for the means of subsistence consumed during the production, and the other as surplus value–value over and above this. If I. has had more outlay it is made up to him by the greater value of his commodity, which replaces this "constant" part, and he has consequently a larger part of the total value to exchange back into the material elements of this constant part; whilst if II. obtains less he has, on the other hand, the less to exchange back. *Differences in rates of profit would therefore, under this assumption, be a matter of indifference,* just as it is today a matter of indifference to the wage-earner by what rate of profit the amount of surplus value squeezed out of him is represented, and just as in international commerce the difference in the rates of profit in the different nations is a matter of indifference for the exchange of their commodities" (iii. 154 seq.).

And now Marx passes at once from the hypothetical style of "supposition" with its subjunctive moods to a series of quite positive conclusions. "The exchange of commodities at their values, or approximately at their values, demands, *therefore,* a much lower stage of development than the exchange into prices of production," ... and "it is, therefore altogether in keeping with fact to regard the values as not only theoretically but *historically* prior to the prices of production. It holds good for circumstances where the means of production belong to the worker, and these circumstances are found both *in the old and in the modern world,* in the cases of peasants who own land and work it themselves, and in the case of artisans" (iii. 155, 156).

What are we to think of this reasoning? I beg the reader above everything to notice carefully that the hypothetical part describes very consistently how exchange would present itself in those primitive conditions of society *if* everything took place according to the Marxian law of value; but that this description contains no shadow of proof, or even of an attempt at proof, that under the given assumptions things must so take place. Marx relates, "supposes," asserts, but he gives no word of proof. He consequently makes a bold, not to say naive jump, when he proclaims as an ascertained result (as though he had successfully worked out a line of argument) that it is, *therefore,* quite consistent with facts to regard values, historically also, as prior to prices of production. As a matter of fact it is beyond question that Marx has not proved by his "supposition" the historical existence of such a condition. He has only hypothetically deduced it from his theory; and as to the credibility of that hypothesis we must, of course, be free to form our own judgment.

As a fact, whether we regard it from within or from without, the gravest doubts arise as to its credibility. It is inherently improbable, and so far as there can be a question here of proof by experience, even experience is against it.

It is inherently altogether improbable. For it requires that it should be a matter of complete indifference to the producers at what time they receive the reward of their activity, and that is economically and psychologically impossible. Let us make this clear to ourselves by considering Marx's own example point by point. Marx compares two workers–I. and II. Labourer No. I. represents a branch of production which requires technically a relatively large and valuable means of production resulting from previous labour, raw material, tools, and auxiliary material. Let us suppose, in order to illustrate the example by figures, that the production of the previous material required five years' labour, whilst the working of it up into finished products was effected in a sixth year. Let us further suppose–what is certainly not contrary to the spirit of the Marxian hypothesis, which is meant to describe very primitive conditions–that labourer No. I. carries on both works, that he both creates the previous material and also works it up into finished products. In these circumstances he will obviously recompense himself for the previous labour of the first years out of the sale of the finished products, which cannot take place till the end of the sixth year. Or, in other words, he will have to wait five years for the return to the first year's work. For the return to the second year he will have to wait four years; for the third year, three years, and so on. Or, taking the average of the six years' work, he will have to wait nearly three years after the work has been accomplished for the return to his labour. The second worker, on the other hand, who represents a branch of production which needs a relatively small means of production resulting from previous labour will perhaps turn out the completed product, taking it through all its stages, in the course of a month, and will therefore receive his compensation from the yield of his product almost immediately after the accomplishment of his work.

Now Marx's hypothesis assumes that the prices of the commodities I. and II. are determined exactly in proportion to the amounts of labour expended in their production, so that the product of six years' work in the commodity No. I. only fetches as much as the total produce of six years' work in commodity No. II. And further, it follows from this that the labourer in commodity No. I. should be satisfied to receive for every year's work, with an average of three years' *delay* of payment, the *same* return that the labourer in commodity No. II. receives *without any delay;* that therefore delay in the receipt of payment is a circumstance which has no part to play in the Marxian hypothesis, and more especially has no influence on competition, on the crowding or understocking of the trade in the different branches of production, having regard to the longer or shorter periods of waiting to which they are subjected.

I leave the reader to judge whether this is probable. In other respects Marx acknowledges that the special accompanying circumstances peculiar to the work of a particular branch of production, the special intensity, strain, or unpleasantness of a work, force a compensation for themselves in the rise of wages through the action of competition. Should not a year's postponement of the remuneration of labour be a circumstance demanding compensation? And further, granting that all producers *would* as soon wait three years for the reward of their labour, as not at all, *could* they really all wait? Marx certainly assumes that "the labourers should possess their respective means of production"; but he does not and cannot venture to assume that each labourer possesses the amount of means of production which are necessary to carry on that branch of industry which for technical reasons requires the command of the greatest quantity of means of production. The different branches of production are therefore certainly not equally accessible to all producers. Those branches of production which demand the least advance of means of production are the most generally accessible, and the branches which demand larger capital are possible only for an increasingly smaller minority. Has this nothing to do with the circumstance that, in the latter branches, a certain restriction in supply takes place, which eventually forces the price of their products above the proportionate level of those branches in the carrying on of which the odious accompaniment of waiting does not enter and which are therefore accessible to a much wider circle of competitors?

Marx himself seems to have been aware that his case contains a certain improbability. He notes first of all, as I have done, though in another form, that the fixing of prices solely in proportion to the amount of labour in the commodities leads in another direction to a disproportion. He asserts this in the form (which is also correct) that the "surplus value" which the labourers in both branches of production obtain over and above their necessary maintenance, calculated on the means of production advanced, shows *unequal rates of profit.* The question naturally obtrudes itself–Why should not this inequality be made to disappear by competition just as in "capitalistic" society? Marx feels the necessity of giving an answer to this, and here only does something of the nature of an attempt to give proofs instead of mere assertions come in. Now what is his answer?

The essential point (he says) is that both labourers should receive the same surplus value for the same working time; or, to be more exact, that for the *same working time"* they should receive the *same values* after deducting the value of the advanced constant element," and on this assumption the difference in the rates of profit would be a "matter of indifference, just as it is a matter of indifference to the wages-earner by what rate of profit the quantity of surplus value squeezed out of him is represented."

Is this a happy simile? If I do not get a thing, then it may certainly be a matter of indifference to me whether that thing, which I do not get, estimated on the capital of another person, represents a higher or lower percentage. But when I get a thing as a settled right, as the worker, on the non-capitalistic hypothesis, is supposed to get the surplus value as profit, then it certainly is not a matter of indifference to me by what scale that profit is to be measured or distributed. It may, perhaps, be an open question whether this profit should be measured and distributed according to the expenditure of labour or to the amount of the advanced means of production, but the question itself can certainly not be a merely indifferent matter to the persons interested in it. And, when, therefore, the somewhat improbable fact is affirmed that unequal rates of profit can exist permanently side by side without being equalised by competition, the reason for this certainly cannot be found in the assumption that the height of the rate of profit is a matter of no importance whatever to the persons interested in it.

But are the labourers on the Marxian hypothesis treated alike even as labourers? They obtain for the same working time the same value and surplus value as wages, but they get it at different times. One obtains it immediately after the completion of the work; the other may have to wait years for the remuneration of his labour. Is this really equal treatment? Or does not the condition under which the remuneration is obtained constitute an inequality which cannot be a matter of indifference to the labourers, but which, on the contrary, as experience truly shows, they feel very keenly? To what worker to-day would it be a matter of indifference whether he received his weekly wages on Saturday evening, or a year, or three years hence? And such marked inequalities would not be smoothed away by competition. That is an improbability for the explanation of which Marx still remains in our debt.

His hypothesis, however, is not only inherently improbable, but it is also contrary to all the facts of experience. It is true that as regards the assumed case, in its full typical purity, we have, after all, no direct experience; for a condition of things in which paid labour is absent and every producer is the independent possessor of his own means of production can now no longer anywhere be seen in its full purity. Still, however, conditions and relationships are found in the "modern world," which correspond at least approximately to those assumed in the Marxian hypothesis. They are found, as Marx himself especially indicates (iii. 156), in the case of the peasant proprietor, who himself cultivates his own land, and in the case of the artisan. According to the Marxian hypothesis, it ought to be a matter of observation that the incomes of these persons did not in the least depend on the amounts of capital they employed in production. They should each receive the same amount of wages and surplus value, whether the capital representing their means of production was 10 shillings or 10,000 shillings. I think, however, that my readers will all allow that though indeed in the cases just mentioned there is no such exact book-keeping as to make it possible to determine proportions with mathematical exactitude, yet the prevailing impression does not confirm Marx's hypothesis, but tends, on the contrary, to the view that in general and as a whole an ampler income is yielded by those branches of industry in which work is carried on with a considerable capital, than by those which have at their disposal only the hands of the producers.

And finally this result of the appeal to fact, which is unfavourable to the Marxian hypothesis, receives trot a little indirect confirmation from the fact that in the second cast: which he instances (a case much easier to test), in which, according to the Marxian theory, the law of value ought to be seen to be completely dominant, no trace of the process alleged by Marx is to be found.

Marx tells us, as we know, that even in a fully developed economy the equalisation of the originally different rates of profit can be brought about only through the action of competition. "If the commodities are sold according to their values," he writes in the most explicit of the passages concerning this matter, [7] "very different rates of profit, as has been explained, occur in the different spheres of production, according to the different organic compositions of the amounts of capital invested in them. But capital withdraws itself from a sphere having a lower rate of profit, and throws itself into another which yields a higher profit. By this constant shifting from one sphere to another–in short, by its distribution among the different spheres according as the rate of profit rises in one and sinks in another–it brings about such a proportion between supply and demand that the average profit in the different spheres of production becomes the same."

We should therefore logically expect,wherever this competition of capital was absent, or was at any rate not yet in full activity, that the original mode of forming prices and profits affirmed by Marx would be met with in its full, or nearly its full, purity. In other words, there must be traces of the actual fact that *before* the equalisation of the rates of profit the branches of production with the relatively greater amounts of constant capital have won and do win the smallest rates of profit, while those branches with the smaller amounts of constant capital will the largest rates of profit. As a matter of fact, however, there are no traces of this to be found anywhere, either in the historical past or in the present. This has been recently so convincingly demonstrated by a learned professor who is in other respects extremely favourable to Marx, that I cannot do better than simply quote the words of Werner Sombart :–

"Development never has and never does take place in the way alleged. If it did it would certainly be seen in operation in the case of at least every new branch of business. If this idea were true, in considering historically the advance of capitalism, one would have to think of it as first occupying those spheres in which living labour preponderated and where, therefore, the composition of capital was under the average (little constant and much variable), and then as passing slowly into other spheres, according to the degree in which prices had fallen in those first spheres in consequence of over production. In a sphere having a preponderance of [material] means of production over living labour, capitalism would naturally in the beginning have realised so small a profit, being limited to the surplus value created by the individual, that it would have had no inducement to enter into that sphere. But capitalistic production at the beginning of its historical development occurs even to some extent in branches of production of the latter kind, mining, &c. Capital would have had no reason to go out of the sphere of circulation in which it was prospering, into the sphere of production, without a prospect of a 'customary profit' which, be it observed, existed in commercial profit previous to any capitalistic production. But we can also show the error of the assumption from the other side. If extremely high profits were obtained in the beginning of capitalistic production, in the spheres having a preponderance of living labour, it would imply that all at once capital had made use of the class of producers concerned (who had up to that time been independent), as wages-earners, i.e., at half the amount of gain they had hitherto procured, and had put the difference in the prices of the commodities, corresponding directly to the values, in its own pocket; and further it supposes, what is an altogether visionary idea, that capitalistic production began with unclassed individuals in branches of production, some of which were quite new creations, and therefore was able to fix prices according to its own standard.

"But if the assumption of an empirical connection between rates of profit and rates of surplus value is false historically, i.e., false as regards the beginning of capitalism, it is even more so as regards conditions in which the capitalistic system of production is fully developed. Whether the composition of a capital by means of which a trade is carried on to-day is ever so high or ever so low, the prices of its products and the calculation (and realisation) of the profits are based solely on the outlay of capital.

"If in all times, earlier as well as later, capitals did, as a matter of fact, pass continually from one sphere of production to another, the principal cause of this would certainly lie in the inequality of profits. But this inequality most surely proceeds not from the organic composition of the capital, but from some cause connected with competition. Those branches of production which to-day flourish more than any others are just those with capitals of very high composition, such as mining, chemical manufactories, breweries, steam mills, &c. Are these the spheres from which capital has withdrawn and migrated until production has been proportionately limited and prices have risen " [8]

These statements will provide matter for many inferences against the Marxian theory. For the present I draw only one which bears immediately on the argument, which is the subject of our inquiry:– the law of value, which, it is conceded, must give up its alleged control over prices of production in an economy where competition is in full force, has never exercised and could never exercise a real sway even in primitive conditions.

We have now seen, wrecked in succession, three contentions which affirmed the existence of certain reserved areas under the immediate control of the law of value. The application of the law of value to the sum total of all commodities and prices of commodities instead of to their several exchange relations (first argument) has been proved to be pure nonsense. The movement of prices (second argument) does not really obey the alleged law of value, and just as little does it exercise a real influence in "primitive conditions" (third argument). There is only one possibility left. Does the law of value, which has no real immediate power anywhere, have perhaps an indirect control, a sort of suzerainty? Marx does not omit to assert this also. It is the subject of the fourth argument, to which we now proceed.

FOURTH ARGUMENT

This argument has been often hinted at by Marx, but so far as I can see he has explained it with any approach to fulness in one place only. The essence of it is this–that the "prices of production," which govern the actual formation of prices, are for their part in their turn under the influence of the law of value, which therefore, through the prices of production, governs the actual exchange relations. The values are "behind the prices of production and determine them in the last resort" (iii. 188). The prices of production are, as Marx often expresses it, only "changed values" or "changed forms of value" (iii. 142, 147, 152 and often). The nature and degree of the influence which the law of value exercises on the prices of production are more clearly explained, however, in a passage on pages 158 and 159. *"The average rate of profit which determines the price of production must,* however, always be approximately equal to the amount of surplus value which falls to a given capital as an aliquot part of the total social capital...Now, as the total value of the commodities governs the total surplus value, and this again determines the amount of the average profit and consequently the general rate of profit–as a general law or a law governing fluctuation–the *law of value regulates the prices of production."*

Let us examine this line of argument point by point.

Marx says at the outset that the average rate of profit determines the prices of production. In Marx's sense this is correct but not complete. Let us make the connection quite clear.

The price of production of a commodity is first of all composed of the "cost price" to the employer of the means of production and of the average profit on the capital employed. The cost price of the means of production consists again of two component parts: the outlay of variable capital, i.e., the money immediately paid in wages, and the outlay for consumed or used up constant capital--raw material, machines, and such-like. As Marx rightly explains, on pages 138 seq., 144, and 186, in a society in which the values have already been changed into prices of production, the purchase or cost price of these means of production does not correspond with their value but with the total amount which has been expended by the producers of these means of production in wages and material appliances, plus the average profit on this expenditure. If we continue this analysis we come at last–as does Adam Smith in his *natural price,* with which, indeed, Marx expressly identifies his price of production (iii. 178),–to resolve the price of production into two components or determinants: (I) the sum total of the wages paid during the different stages of production, which taken altogether represent the actual cost price of the commodities; [9] and (2) the sum total of the *profits* on all these wage outlays calculated *pro rata temporis,* and according to the average rate of profit.

Undoubtedly, therefore, *one* determinant of the price of production of a commodity is the average profit incidental to its production. Or the other determinant, the total of wages paid, Marx speaks no further in this passage. In another place, however, to which we have alluded, he says in a very general way that "the values stand behind the prices of production," and "that the law of value determines these latter in the last resort." In order to avoid a hiatus, therefore, we must subject this second factor also to our scrutiny and judge accordingly whether it can rightly be said to be determined by the law of value, and, if so, in what degree.

It is evident that the total expenditure in wages is a product of the quantity of labour employed multiplied by the average rate of the wages. Now as, according to the [Marxian] law of value, the exchange relations must be determined solely by the quantity of labour employed, and Marx repeatedly and most emphatically denies that the rate of wages has any influence on the value of the commodities, [10] it is also evident that, of the two components of the factor expenditure in wages, only the amount of labour employed is in harmony with the law of value, whilst in the second component, rate of wages, a determinant alien to the law of value enters among the determinants of the prices of production.

The nature and degree of the operation of this determinant may be illustrated, in order to avoid all misunderstanding, by one other example. Let us take three commodities–A, B, and C–which, to begin with, have the same production price of 100 shillings, but which are of different types of composition as regards the elements of their cost. Let us further suppose that the wages for a day amount at first to five shillings, and the rate of surplus value, or the degree of exploitation, to 100%, so that from the total value of the commodities of 300 shillings, 150 falls to wages and another 150 to surplus value; and that the total capital (invested in different proportions in the three commodities) amounts to 1,500 shillings. The average rate of profit would therefore be 10%· The following table illustrates this assumption:–

Commodity	Expended Time	Expended Wages	Capital Employed	Average profit accruing	Production price
A	10	50s	500s	50s	100s
B	6	30s	700s	70s	100s
C	14	70s	300s	30s	100s
Totals -	30	150s	1,500s	150s	300s

Now let us assume a rise in the wages from five to six shillings. According to Marx this can only take place at the expense of the surplus value, other conditions remaining the same. Therefore of the total product of 300 shillings, which remains unaltered, there will fall (owing to a diminution in the degree of exploitation) 180 to wages and only 120 to surplus value, and consequently the average rate of profit on the capital employed falls to 8%. The following table shows the changes which take place, in consequence, in the compositions of the elements of capital and in the prices of production:–

Commodity	Expended Time	Expended Wages	Capital Employed	Average profit accruing	Production price
A	10	60s	500s	40s	100s
B	6	36s	700s	56s	92s
C	14	84s	300s	242s	108s
Totals -	30	180s	1,500s	120s	300s

It appears from this that a rise in wages, when the amount of labour remains the same, brings with it a material alteration in the originally equal prices of production and relations of exchange. The alteration can be partly, but obviously not altogether, traced to the contemporaneous necessary change produced in the average rate of profit by the alteration in the wages. I say "obviously not altogether," because the price of production of commodity C, for example, has really *risen* in spite of the fall in the amount of profit contained in it, therefore this change of price cannot be brought about by the change of profit *only*. I raise this really obvious point merely in order to show that in the rate of wages we have, indisputably, a price-determinant which does not exhaust its force in its influence on the rate of profit, but also exerts a special and direct influence; and that therefore we have reason to submit this particular price determinant–which is passed over by Marx in the passage cited above–to a separate consideration. The summary of the results of this consideration I reserve for a later stage, and in the meantime we will examine step by step Marx's assertion concerning the way in which the second determinant of the price of production, the average profit, is regulated by the law of value.

The connection is anything but a direct one. It is effected by the following links in his line of reasoning, some of which are indicated only elliptically by Marx, but which undoubtedly enter into his argument:–The *law of value* determines the *aggregate value* of the whole of the commodities produced in the society; [11] the *aggregate value* of the commodities determines the *aggregate surplus value* contained in them; the latter distributed over the total social capital determines the *average rate of profit:* this rate applied to the capital employed in the production of a single commodity gives the *concrete average profit,* which finally enters as an element into the price of production of the commodity in question. In this way the first link in this sequence, the *law of value,* regulates the last link, *the price of production.*

Now for our running commentary on this series of arguments.

1. We are struck by the fact which must be kept in mind, that Marx after all does not affirm that there is a connection between the average profit entering into the price of production of the commodities and the values incorporated in single commodities by reason of the law of value. On the contrary, he says emphatically in numerous places that the amount of surplus value which enters into the price of production of a commodity is independent of and indeed fundamentally different from "the surplus value actually created in the sphere in which the separate commodity is produced" (iii. 146; similarly iii. 144, and often). He therefore does not after all connect the influence ascribed to the law of value with the characteristic function of the law of value, in virtue of which this law determines the exchange relations of the *separate commodities,* but only with another assumed function (concerning the highly problematical nature of which we have already passed an opinion), viz., the determination of the aggregate value of *all commodities taken together.* In this application, as we have convinced ourselves, the law of value has no meaning whatever. If the idea and the law of value are to be brought to bear–and Marx certainly means that they should–on the exchange relations of goods, [12] then there is no sense in applying the idea and law to an aggregate which as such cannot be subject to those relations. As no exchange of this aggregate takes place, there is naturally neither a measure nor a determinant for its exchange, and therefore it cannot give material for a "law of value." If, however, the law of value has no real influence at all on a chimerical "aggregate value of all commodities taken together," there can be no further application of its influence to other relations, and the whole logical series which Marx endeavoured to work out with such seeming cogency hangs therefore in the air.

2. But let us turn away altogether from this first fundamental defect, and let us independently of it test the strength of the other arguments in the series. Let us assume, therefore, that the aggregate value of the commodities is a real quantity, and actually determined by the law of value. The second argument affirms that this aggregate value of commodities determines the aggregate surplus value. Is this true?

The surplus value, unquestionably, represents no fixed or unalterable quota of the total national product, but is the difference between the "aggregate value" of the national product and the amount of the wages paid to the workers. That aggregate value, therefore, does not in any case rule the amount of the total surplus value by itself alone. It can at the most supply only one determinant of its amount, by the side of which stands a second, alien determinant, the rate of wages. But, it may be asked, does not this also, perhaps, obey the Marxian law of value?

In the first volume Marx had still unconditionally affirmed this. " The value of labour," he writes on page 155, "is determined, like that of every other commodity, by the working time necessary to the production, and therefore also reproduction, of this specific article." And on the next page he proceeds to define this proposition more fully: "For his maintenance the living individual needs a certain amount of means of subsistence. The working time necessary to the production of the labour power resolves itself, therefore, into the working time necessary to the production of these means of subsistence, or the value of the labour power is the value of the means of subsistence necessary to the maintenance of its possessor." In the third volume Marx, however, is forced considerably to modify this statement Thus, on page 186 of that volume, he rightly draws attention to the fact that it is possible that the necessary means of subsistence of the labourer also can be sold at prices of production which deviate from that of the necessary working time. In such a case, Marx says, the variable part of the capital (i.e., the wages paid) may also deviate from its value. In other words, the wages (apart from purely temporary oscillations) may permanently deviate from the rate which should correspond to the quantity of work incorporated in the necessary means of subsistence, or to the strict requirements of the law of value. Therefore at least *one* determinant alien to the law of value is already a factor in determining the total surplus value.

3. The factor, aggregate surplus value, thus determined, "regulates," according to Marx, the average rate of profit, but obviously only in so far as the aggregate surplus value furnishes one determinant, whilst another–the amount of capital existing in a given society–acts as a second determinant, entirely independent of the first and of the law of value. If, as in the above table, the total surplus value is 150 shillings, the surplus value being 100%, then, if and because the total capital expended in all its branches of production amounts to 1,500 shillings, the rate of profit amounts to 10%. If the total surplus value remained exactly the same, but the total capital participating in it amounted to 3,000 shillings, the rate of profit would obviously amount only to 5%; and it would be fully 20% if the total capital amounted only to 750 shillings. It is obvious, therefore, that again a determinant enters into the chain of influence which is entirely alien to the law of value.

4. We must, therefore, further conclude that the average rate of profit regulates the amount of the concrete average profit which accrues from the production of a special commodity. But this, again, is only true with the same restrictions as in the former arguments of the series. That is to say, the total amount of the average profit which accrues from the production of a separate commodity is the product of two factors: the quantity of invested capital multiplied by the average rate of profit. The quantity of the capital to be invested in the different stages is again determined by two factors, namely, by the quantity of the work to be remunerated (a factor which is of course not out of harmony with Marx's law of value), and also by the rate of wages to be paid; and with this latter factor, as we have just convinced ourselves, a factor alien to the law of value comes into play.

5. In the next argument of the series we go back again to the beginning: the average profit (defined in the fourth argument) must regulate the price of production of the commodity. This is true with the correction that the average profit is only one factor determining prices side by side with the expended wages in which, as we have repeatedly stated, there is an element, which is foreign to Marx's law of value, and which co-operates in determining prices.

Let us sum up. What is the proposition which Marx undertook to prove? It ran thus: "The law of value regulates the prices of production," or as otherwise stated, "The values determine in the last resort the prices of production," or if we formulate the meaning which Marx himself attached to value and law of value in the first volume the statement is: Prices of production are governed "in the last resort" by the principle that the quantity of labour is the only condition which determines the exchange relations of commodities.

And what do we find on examining the separate links of the argument? We find that the price of production is, first of all, made up of two components. One, the expended wages, is the product of two factors, of which the first–the quantity of work–is in harmony with the substance of the Marxian "value," and the other–the rate of wages–is not. Marx himself could only affirm of the second component–the total amount of accruing average profit–that it was connected with the law of value by means of a violent perversion of this law, alleging its operation in a domain in which no exchange relations exist at all. But apart from this, the factor "aggregate value of commodities " which Marx wishes to deduce from the law of value must, in any case, co-operate in determining the next link, the aggregate surplus value, along with a factor, "rate of wages," which is no longer homogeneous with the law of value. The "aggregate surplus value" would have to co-operate with a completely foreign element, the mass of social capital, in determining the average rate of profit;

and, finally, the latter would have to co-operate with a partially foreign element, expended wages, in determining the accruing total profit.

The factor "aggregate value of all commodities," booked with doubtful correctness to the credit of the Marxian law of value, consequently co-operates after a triple homoeopathic dilution of its influence (and naturally, therefore, with a share of influence diminished in proportion to this dilution) in determining the average profit, and also the prices of production. The following would, therefore, be a sober statement of the facts of the case. The quantity of labour which, according to the Marxian law of value, must entirely and exclusively govern the exchange relations of commodities proves itself as a matter of fact to be only one determinant of the prices of production side by side with other determinants. It has a strong, a tolerably direct influence on the one component of prices of production which consists of expended wages; a much more remote, weak, and, for the most part, [13] even problematical influence upon the second component, the average profit.

Now, I ask, do we find in this condition of things a confirmation or a contradiction of the claim that, in the last resort, the law of value determines the prices of production? I do not think that there can be a moment's doubt as to the answer. The law of value maintains that quantity of labour alone determines the exchange relations; facts show that it is *not* only the quantity of labour, or the factors in harmony with it, which determine the exchange relations. These two propositions bear the same relation to each other as Yes to No–as affirmation to contradiction. Whoever accepts the second proposition–and Marx's theory of the prices of production involves this acceptance–contradicts *de facto* the first. And if Marx really could have thought that he did not contradict himself and his first proposition, he allowed himself to be deluded by some strange mistake. He could not have seen that it is very different for one factor involved in a law to have some sort and degree of influence and for the law itself to be in full force.

The most trivial example will perhaps serve best in so obvious a matter. Suppose a discussion on the effect of cannon-balls on iron-clad vessels, and some one says that the degree of destructive power in the balls is due solely to the amount of powder with which the cannon is charged. When this statement is questioned and tested by actual experience it is seen that the effect of the shot is not due only to the amount of gunpowder in the charge, but also to the strength of the powder; and, further, to the construction, length, &c., of the barrel of the gun, the form and hardness of the balls, the distance of the object, and last, but not least, to the thickness and firmness of the plates on the vessel.

And now after all this has been conceded, could it still be said that nevertheless the first statement was true, because it had been proved that the alleged factor, the amount of gunpowder, does exert an important influence on the discharge, and that this was proved by the fact that, other circumstances being equal, the effect of the shot would be greater or less in proportion to the amount of gunpowder used in the charge.

This is what Marx does. He declares most emphatically that nothing can be at the root of exchange relations but quantity of labour alone; he argues strenuously with the economists who acknowledge other determinants of value and price besides the quantity of labour–the influence of which on the exchange value of goods freely reproduced no one denies. From the exclusive position of quantity of labour as the sole determinant of exchange relations he deduces in two volumes the most weighty and practical conclusions–his theory of surplus value and his denunciation of the capitalistic organisation of society–in order, in the third volume, to develop a theory of prices of production which substantially recognises the influence of other determinants as well. But instead of thoroughly analysing these other determinants, he always lays his finger triumphantly on the points where his idol, quantity of labour, either actually, or in his opinion, exerts an influence; on such points as the change in prices when the amount of labour changes, the influence of "aggregate value" on average rate of profit, &c. He is silent about the co-ordinate influence of foreign determinants as well as about the influence of the amount of social capital on the rate of profit, and about the alteration of prices through a change in the organic composition of the capital, or in the rate of wages. Passages in which he recognises these influences are not wanting in his book. The influence of the rate of wages on prices is, for instance, aptly treated of in page 179 seq., then in page 186; the influence of the amount of social capital on the height of the average rate of profit in pages 145, 184, 191 seq., 197 seq., 203, and often; the influence of the organic composition of capital on the prices of production in pages 142 seq. It is characteristic that in the passages devoted to the justification of his law of value Marx passes silently over these other influences, and only mentions in a one-sided way the part played by quantity of labour, in order to deduce from the first and undisputed premise, that quantity of labour co-operates at many points to determine the prices of production, the utterly unjustifiable conclusion that, in the "last resort," the law of value, which proclaims the sole dominion of labour, determines the prices of production. This is to evade the admission of the contradiction; it is not to escape from the contradiction itself.

[1] *Geschichte und Kritik der Kapitalzinstheorieen.* Innsbruck, 1884, p. 413. Translation, p. 362.
[2] See his work, *Die Durchschnittsprofitrate auf Grundlage des Marxschen Wertgesetzes,* Stuttgart, 1889, especially section 13; and my review of this work in the *Tubinger Zeitschrift f. d. ges. Staatswissenschaft,* 1890, pp. 590 seq.
[3] *L'opera postuma ai Carlo Marx, Nuova Antologia,* February 1, 1895, pp. 20, 22, 23.
[4] *Zur Ktitik des Okonomischen Systems von Karl Marx,* in the *Archiv fur sociale Gesetzgebung,* vol. vii., part 4, pp. 571 seq.
[5] See his work quoted above, especially section 13.
[6] III. 156, and quite similarly in the passage already quoted, iii. 158.

[7] III. 175 seq. Compare also the shorter statements, iii. 136, 151, 159, and frequently.

[8] Zut Kritik des ok, Systems von Karl Marx, Archiv fur sociale Gesetzgebung, vol. vii. pp. 584-6. I am bound, however, to make it clear that in the passage quoted Sombart intended to combat Marx, only on the assumption that Marx's doctrines did actually have the meaning attributed to them in the text. He himself ascribes to them, in his "attempt at rescue," already referred to by me, another, and, as I think, a somewhat exotic meaning, which I shall discuss in detail later on.

[9] "The cost price of a commodity refers only to the amount of paid labour contained in it" (Marx iii. 144).

[10] For instance iii. 187, where Marx affirms "that in no circumstances can the rise or fall of wages ever affect the value of the commodities."

[11] This link is not expressly inserted by Marx in the passage quoted. Its insertion is nevertheless self-evident.

[12] As I have already mentioned, I shall take special notice by and by of the different view of W. Sombart.

[13] In so far, namely, as it is supposed to be brought about by the factor "aggregate value," which, in my opinion, has nothing to do with the embodied amount of labour. As, however, the factor "expended wages" (in determining which the amount of work to be remunerated certainly co-operates as an element) also appears in the following links, the amount of work always finds a place among the indirect determinants of average profit.

Chapter Four - The Error in the Marxian System - Its Origin and Ramifications

Section One

THE evidence that an author has contradicted himself may be a necessary stage, but it cannot be the ultimate aim of a fruitful and well directed criticism. To be aware that there is a defect in a system, which may possibly be accidental only and peculiar to the author, requires a comparatively low degree of critical intelligence. A firmly rooted system can only be effectually overthrown by discovering with absolute precision the point at which the error made its way into the system and the manner in which it spread and branched itself out. As opponents we ought to study the beginning, the development, and the final issue of the error which culminates in self-contradiction as thoroughly, I might almost say as sympathetically, as we would study the connection of a system with which we were in agreement.

Owing to many peculiar circumstances the question of self-contradiction has, in the case of Marx, gained a more than ordinary importance, and consequently I have devoted a considerable space to it. But in dealing with a thinker so important and influential as Marx it is incumbent upon us to apply ourselves to the second and, in this case as I think, the actually more fruitful and instructive part of the criticism.

We will begin with a question which will carry us straight to the main point: In what way did Marx arrive at the fundamental proposition of his teaching–the proposition that all value depends solely upon incorporated quantities of labour?

That this proposition is not a self-evident axiom, needing no proof, is beyond doubt. Value and effort, as I have stated at length in another place, are not ideas so intimately connected that one is forced immediately to adopt the view that effort is the basis of value. "That I have toiled over a thing is one fact, that the thing is worth the toil is another and a different fact, and that the two facts do not always go hand in hand is far too firmly established by experience to admit of any doubt. It is proved by all the labour which is daily wasted on valueless results, owing either to want of technical skill, or to bad speculation, or to simple misfortune; and not less by each of the numerous cases in which a very little toil has a result of very great value." [1]

When therefore it is affirmed that a necessary and natural correspondence between value and effort exists in any quarter, it behooves us to give ourselves and our readers some grounds in support of such a statement.

Now Marx himself advances proofs of it in his system; but I think I shall be able to convince my readers that from the outset his line of argument is unnatural and not suited to the character of the problem; and further that the evidence which Marx advances in his system is clearly not the same as that by means of which he himself arrives at his convictions, but was thought out subsequently as an artificial support for an opinion which was previously derived from other sources; and finally–and this is the most decisive point–that the reasoning is full of the most obvious faults of logic and method which deprive it of all cogency.

Let us examine this more closely.

The fundamental proposition which Marx puts before his readers is that the exchange value of commodities–for his analysis is directed only to this, not to value in use–finds its origin and its measure in the quantity of labour incorporated in the commodities.

Now it is certain that the exchange values, that is to say the prices of the commodities as well as the quantities of labour which are necessary for their reproduction, are real, external quantities, which on the whole it is quite possible to determine empirically. Obviously, therefore, Marx ought to have turned to experience for the proof of a proposition the correctness or incorrectness of which must be manifested in the facts of experience; or in other words, he should have given a purely empirical proof in support of a proposition adapted to a purely empirical proof. This, however, Marx does not do. And one cannot even say that he heedlessly passes by this possible and certainly proper source of knowledge and conviction. The reasoning of the third volume proves that he was quite aware of the nature of the empirical facts, and that they were opposed to his proposition. He knew that the prices of commodities were not in proportion to the amount of incorporated labour, but to the total cost of production, which comprise other elements besides. He did not therefore accidentally overlook this the most natural proof of his proposition, but turned away from it with the full consciousness that upon this road no issue favourable to his theory could be obtained.

But there is yet another and perfectly natural way of testing and proving such propositions, viz., the psychological. We can by a combination of induction and deduction, much used in our science, investigate the motives which direct people in carrying on the business of exchange and in determining exchange prices on the one hand, and on the other hand which guide them in their co-operation in production; and from the nature of these motives a typical mode of action may be inferred through which, among other things, it is conceivable that a connection should result between the regularly demanded and accepted prices and the quantity of work necessary for the production of the commodities. This method has often been followed with the best results in exactly similar questions–for instance, the usual justification of the law of supply and demand and of the law of costs of production, and the explanation of ground rents, rests upon it. And Marx himself, in a general way at least, has often made use of it; but just in dealing with his fundamental proposition he avoids it. Although, obviously, the affirmed external connection between exchange relations and quantities of work could only be fully understood by the discovery of the psychological links which connect the two, he foregoes all explanation of these internal connections. He even once says, incidentally, that "the deeper analysis" of the two social forces, "demand and supply"–which would have led to this internal connection–"is not apposite here " (iii. 169), where the "here" refers only to a digression on the influence of supply and demand on the formation of prices. In reality, however, nowhere in the whole Marxian system is a really "deep" and thorough analysis attempted; and most of all is the absence of this analysis noticeable where he is preparing the ground for his most important leading idea.

But here again we notice something strange. Marx does not, as might have been expected, pass over this second possible and natural method of investigation with an easy carelessness. He studiously avoids it, and with a full consciousness of what the results of following it would be, and that they would not be favourable to his thesis. In the third volume, for instance, he actually brings forward, under their roughly collective name of "competition," those motives operative in production and exchange, the "deeper analysis" of which he foregoes here and elsewhere, and demonstrates that these motives do not in reality lead to an adjustment of the prices to the quantities of labour incorporated in the commodities, but that, on the contrary, they force them away from this level to a level which implies at least one other co-ordinating factor. Indeed it is competition which, according to Marx, leads to the formation of the celebrated average rate of profit and to the "transfer" of pure labour values into prices of production, which differ from them and contain a portion of average profit.

Now Marx, instead of proving his thesis from experience or from its operant motives–that is, empirically or psychologically–prefers another, and for such a subject somewhat singular line of evidence–the method of a purely logical proof, a dialectic deduction from the very nature of exchange. Marx had found in old Aristotle the idea that "exchange cannot exist without equality, and equality cannot exist without commensurability" (i. 35). Starting with this idea he expands it. He conceives the exchange of two commodities under the form of an equation, and from this infers that "a common factor of the same amount" must exist in the things exchanged and thereby equated, and then proceeds to search for this common factor to which the two equated things must as exchange values be "reducible" (i. 11).

I should like to remark, in passing, that the first assumption, according to which an "equality" must be manifested in the exchange of two things, appears to me to be very old-fashioned, which would not, however, much were it not also very unrealistic. In plain English, it seems to me to be a wrong idea. Where equality and exact equilibrium obtain, no change is likely to occur to disturb the balance. When, therefore, in the case of exchange the matter terminates with a change of ownership of the commodities, it points rather to the existence of some inequality or preponderance which produces the alteration. When composite bodies are brought into close contact with each other new chemical combinations are produced by some of the constituent elements of one body uniting with those of another body, not because they possess an exactly equal degree of chemical affinity, but because they have a stronger affinity with each other than with the other elements of the bodies to which they originally belonged. So here. And as a matter of fact modern political economists agree that the old scholastico-theological theory of "equivalence" in the commodities to be exchanged is untenable. I will not, however, dwell any longer on this point, but will proceed to the critical investigation of the logical and systematic processes of distillation by means of which Marx obtains the sought-for "common factor" in labour.

It is these processes which appear to me to constitute, as I have before said, the most vulnerable point in the Marxian theory. They exhibit as many cardinal errors as there are points in the arguments–of which there are not a few–and they bear evident traces of having been a subtle and artificial afterthought contrived to make a preconceived opinion seem the natural outcome of a prolonged investigation.

Marx searches for the "common factor" which is the characteristic of exchange value in the following way. He passes in review the various properties possessed by the objects made equal in exchange, and according to the method of exclusion separates all those which cannot stand the test, until at last only one property remains, that of being the product of labour. This, therefore, must be the sought-for common property.

This line of procedure is somewhat singular, but not in itself objectionable. It strikes one as strange that instead of submitting the supposed characteristic property to a positive test–as would have been done if either of the other methods studiously avoided by Marx had been employed–Marx tries to convince us that he has found the sought-for property, by a purely negative proof, viz., by showing that it is not any of the other properties. This method can always lead to the desired end if attention and thoroughness are used–that is to say, if extreme care is taken that everything that ought to be included is actually passed through the logical sieve and that no mistake has been made in leaving anything out.

But how does Marx proceed?

From the beginning he only puts into the sieve those exchangeable things which contain the property which he desires finally to sift out as "the common factor," and he leaves all the others outside. He acts as one who urgently desiring to bring a white ball out of an urn takes care to secure this result by putting in white balls only. That is to say he limits from the outset the field of his search for the substance of the exchange value to "commodities," and in doing so he forms a conception with a meaning narrower than the conception of "goods" (though he does not clearly define it), and limits it to products of labour as against gifts of nature. Now it stands to reason that if exchange really means an equalisation, which assumes the existence of a "common factor of the same amount," this common factor must be sought and found in every species of goods which is brought into exchange, not only in products of labour but also in gifts of nature, such as the soil, wood in trees, water power, coal-beds, stone quarries, petroleum springs, mineral waters, gold mines, &c. [2] To exclude the exchangeable goods which are not products of labour in the search for the common factor which lies at the root of exchange value is, under the circumstances, a great error of method. It is just as though a natural philosopher, desiring to discover a property common to all bodies–weight, for instance–were to sift the properties of a single group of bodies–transparent bodies, for instance–and after passing in review all the properties common to transparent bodies were to declare that transparency must be the cause of weight, for the sole reason that he could demonstrate that it could not be caused by ally of the other properties.

The exclusion of the gifts of nature (which would never have entered the head of Aristotle, the father of the idea of equality in exchange) is the less to be justified because many natural gifts, such as the soil, are among the most important objects of property and commerce, and also because it is impossible to affirm that in nature's gifts exchange values are always established arbitrarily and by accident. On the one hand, there are such things as accidental prices among products of labour; and on the other hand the prices in the case of nature's gifts are frequently shown to be distinctly related to antecedent conditions or determining motives. For instance, that the sale price of land is a multiple of its rent calculated on an interest usual in the country of sale is as well known a fact as that the wood in a tree, or the coal in a pit, brings a higher or lower price according to differences of quality or of distance from market, and not by mere accident.

Marx also takes care to avoid mentioning or explaining the fact that he excludes from his investigation a part of exchangeable goods. In this case, as in many others, he manages to glide with dialectic skill over the difficult points of his argument. He omits to call his readers' attention to the fact that his idea of "commodities" is narrower than that of exchangeable goods as a whole. He very cleverly prepares us for the acceptance of the subsequent limitation of the investigation to commodities by placing at the beginning of his book the apparently harmless general phrase that "the wealth of the society in which a capitalistic system of production is dominant appears as an immense *collection of commodities.*" This proposition is quite wrong if we take the term "commodity" to mean products of labour, which is the sense Marx subsequently gives to it. For the gifts of nature, inclusive of the soil, constitute a by no means insignificant, but on the contrary a very important element of national wealth. The ingenuous reader easily overlooks this inaccuracy, however, for of course he does not know that later Marx will give a much more restricted meaning to the term "commodity."

Nor is this made clear in what immediately follows. On the contrary, in the first paragraphs of the first chapter we read in turns of a "thing," a "value in use," a "good," and a "commodity," without any clear distinction being made between the last and the three former. "The usefulness of a *thing,*" it says on page 10, *"makes it a value in use":* "the commodity ... *is a value in use* or *good.*" On page 11 we read, "Exchange value appears...as the quantitative proportion ... in which *values in use* of one kind exchange with *values in use* of another kind." And here let it be noticed that it is just the value in use = good which is still directly indicated as the main factor of the exchange phenomenon. And with the phrase "Let us look into the matter more closely," which surely cannot be meant to prepare us for a leap into another and a narrower field of research, Marx continues, "a single *commodity,* a quarter of wheat, for instance, exchanges in the most varying proportions with other *articles.*" And "Let us further take two *commodities,*" &c. In the same paragraph the term "things" occurs again, and indeed with the application which is most important for the problem, viz., "that a common factor of equal amount exists in two different *things*" (which are made equal to each other in exchange).

On the next page (p. 12), however, Marx directs his search for the "common factor" only to the "exchange value of *commodities,*" without hinting, even in the faintest whisper, that he has thereby limited the field of research to a part only of the things possessing exchange value. [3] And immediately, on the next page (p. 13), the limitation is again abandoned and the results just obtained in the narrower area are applied to the wider sphere of values in use, or goods. "A *value in use,* or a *good,* has therefore only a value because abstract human labour is stored up or materialised in it."

If Marx had not confined his research, at the decisive point, to products of labour, but had sought for the common factor in the exchangeable gifts of

46

nature as well, it would have become obvious that work cannot be the common factor. If he had carried out this limitation quite clearly and openly this gross fallacy of method would inevitably have struck both himself and his readers; and they would have been forced to laugh at the naive juggle by means of which the property of being a product of labour has been successfully distilled out as the common property of a group from which all exchangeable things which naturally belong to it, and which are not the products of labour, have been first of all eliminated. The trick could only have been performed, as Marx performed it, by gliding unnoticed over the knotty point with a light and quick dialectic. But while I express my sincere admiration of the skill with which Marx managed to present so faulty a mode of procedure in so specious a form, I can of course only maintain that the proceeding itself is altogether erroneous.

But we will proceed. By means of the artifice just described Marx has merely succeeded in convincing us that labour can in fact enter into the competition. And it was only by the artificial narrowing of the sphere that it could even have become *one* "common" property of this narrow sphere. But by its side other properties could claim to be as common. How now is the exclusion of these other competitors effected? It is effected by two arguments, each of a few words only, but which contain one of the most serious of logical fallacies.

In the first of these Marx excludes all "geometrical, physical, chemical, or other natural properties of the commodities," for "their physical properties only come into consideration in so far as they make the commodities useful—make them values in use, therefore. *On the other hand, the exchange relation of commodities evidently involves our disregarding their values in use*"; because "within this relation (the exchange relation) *one value in use is worth exactly as much as every other, provided only it is present in proper proportions* "(i. 12).

In making clear what this argument involves I may be permitted to quote from my History and Criticism of Theories of Capital and Interest (p. 435; Eng. trans., p. 381):

"What would Marx have said to the following argument? In an opera company there are three celebrated singers, a tenor, a bass, and a baritone, each with a salary of £2,000. Some one asks, 'What is the common circumstance on account of which their salaries are made equal?' And I answer, 'In the question of salary one good voice counts for just as much as any other, a good tenor for as much as a good bass or a good baritone, provided only it is to be had in proper proportion. Consequently in the question of salary the good voice is evidently disregarded, and the good voice cannot be the common cause of the high salary.' That this argument is false, is clear. But it is just as clear that Marx's syllogism, from which this is copied, is not an atom more correct. Both commit the same fallacy. They confuse abstraction from the genus, and abstraction from the specific forms in which the genus manifests itself. In our illustration the circumstance which is of no account as regards the question of salary is evidently only the special form in which the good voice appears, whether as tenor, bass, or baritone, and by no means the good voice as such. And just so is it with the exchange relation of commodities. The special forms under which the values in use of the commodities may appear, whether they serve for food, shelter, clothing, &c., is of course disregarded, but the value in use of the commodity as such is never disregarded. Marx might have seen that we do not absolutely disregard value in use, from the fact that there can be no exchange value where there is no value in use--a fact which Marx is himself repeatedly forced to admit." [4] The second step in the argument is still worse: "If the use value of commodities be disregarded"–these are Marx's words–"there remains in them *only one other property, that of being products of labour.*" Is it so? I ask to-day as I asked twelve years ago: Is there only one other property? Is not the property of being scarce in proportion to demand also common to all exchangeable goods? Or that they are the subjects of demand and supply? Or that they are appropriated? Or that they are natural products? For that they are products of nature, just as they are products of labour, no one asserts more plainly than Marx himself, when he declares in one place that "commodities are combinations of two elements, natural material and labour." Or is not the property that they cause expense to their producers–a property to which Marx draws attention in the third volume–common to exchangeable goods?

Why then, I ask again to-day, may not the principle of value reside in any one of these common properties as well as in the property of being products of labour? For in support of this latter proposition Marx has not adduced a shred of positive evidence. His sole argument is the negative one, that the value in use, from which we have happily abstracted, is not the principle of exchange value. But does not this negative argument apply equally to all the other common properties overlooked by Marx? And this is not all. On page 12, in which Marx has abstracted from the influence of the value in use on exchange value by arguing that any one value in use is worth as much as any other if only it is present in proper proportion, he writes as follows about products of labour: "But even as the product of labour they have already changed in our hand. For if we abstract from a commodity its value in use, we at the same time take from it the material constituents and forms which give it a value in use. It is no longer a table, or a house, or yam, or any other useful thing. All its physical qualities have disappeared. *Nor is it any longer the product of the labour of the carpenter, or the mason, or the spinner, or of any other particular productive industry.* With the useful character of the labour products there disappears the useful character of the labour embodied in them, and there vanish also the different concrete forms of those labours. *They are no longer distinguished from each other, but are all reduced to identical human labour–abstract human labour.*"

Is it possible to state more clearly or more emphatically that for an exchange relation not only any one value in use, but also any one kind of labour or product of labour is worth exactly as much as any other, if only it is present in proper proportion? Or, in other words, that exactly the same evidence on which Marx formulated his verdict of exclusion against the value in use holds good with regard to labour. Labour and value in use have a qualitative side and a quantitative side. As the value in use is different qualitatively as table, house, or yarn, so is labour as carpentry, masonry, or spinning. And just as one can compare different kinds of labour according to their quantity, so one can compare values in use of different kinds according to the amount of the value in use. It is quite impossible to understand why the very same evidence should result in the one competitor being excluded and in the other getting the crown and the prize. If Marx had chanced to reverse the order of the examination, the same reasoning which led to the exclusion of the value in use would have excluded labour; and then the reasoning which resulted in the crowning of labour might have led him to declare the value in use to be the only property left, and therefore to be the sought-for common property, and value to be "the cellular tissue of value in use." I think it can be maintained seriously, not in jest, that, if the subjects of the two paragraphs on page 12 were transposed (in the first of which the influence of value in use is thought away, and in the second labour is shown to be the sought-for common factor), the seeming justness of the reasoning would not be affected, that labour and products of labour could be substituted everywhere for value in use in the otherwise unaltered structure of the first paragraph, and that in the structure of the second paragraph value in use could be substituted throughout for labour.

Of such a nature are the reasoning and the method employed by Marx in introducing into his system his fundamental proposition that labour is the sole basis of value. In my opinion it is quite impossible that this dialectical hocus-pocus constituted the ground and source of Marx's own convictions. It would have been impossible for a thinker such as he was (and I look upon him as an intellectual force of the very highest order), to have followed such tortuous and unnatural methods had he been engaged, with a free and open mind, in really investigating the actual connections of things, and in forming his own conclusions with regard to them; it would have been impossible for him to fall successively by mere accident into all the errors of thought and method which I have described, and to arrive at the conclusion that labour is the sole source of value as the natural outgrowth, not the desired and predetermined result, of such a mode of inquiry.

I think the case was really different. That Marx was truly and honestly convinced of the truth of his thesis I do not doubt. But the grounds of his conviction are not those which he gives in his system. They were in reality opinions rather than thought-out conclusions. Above all they were opinions derived from authority. Smith and Ricardo, the great authorities, as was then at least believed, had taught the same doctrine. They had not *proved* it any more than Marx. They had only postulated it from certain general confused impressions. But they explicitly contradicted it when they examined things more closely and in quarters where a closer examination could not be avoided. Smith, in the same way as Marx in his third volume, taught that in a developed economic system values and prices gravitate towards a level of costs which besides labour comprises an average profit of capital. And Ricardo, too, in the celebrated fourth section of the chapter "On Value," clearly and definitely stated that by the side of labour, mediate or immediate, the amount of capital invested and the duration of the investment exercise a determining influence on the value of the goods. In order to maintain without obvious contradiction their cherished philosophical principle that labour is the "true" source of value, they were obliged to beat a retreat to mythical times and places in which capitalists and landed proprietors did not exist. There they could maintain it without contradiction, for there was nothing to restrain them. Experience, which does not support the theory, was not there to refute them. Nor were they restrained by a scientific, psychological analysis, for like Marx they avoided such an analysis. They did not seek to prove—they postulated, as a "natural" state, an idyllic state of things where labour and value were one. [5] It was to tendencies and views of this kind, which had acquired from Smith and Ricardo a great but not undisputed authority, that Marx became heir, and as an ardent socialist he willingly believed in them. It is not surprising that he did not take a more sceptical attitude with regard to a view which was so well adapted to support his economic theory of the world than did Ricardo, to whom it must have gone sorely against the grain. It is not surprising, too, that he did not allow those views of the classical writers which were against him to excite any critical doubts in his own mind on the doctrine that value is wholly labour, but considered that they were only attempts on their part to escape in an indirect way from the unpleasant consequences of an inconvenient truth. In short, it is not surprising that the same material on which the classical writers had grounded their half-confused, half-contradictory, and wholly unproved opinions should have served Marx as foundation for the same assumption, believed in unconditionally and with earnest conviction. For himself he needed no further evidence. Only for his system he needed a formal proof.

It is clear that he could not rely simply on the classical writers for this, as they had not proved anything; and we also know that he could not appeal to experience, or attempt an economico-psychological proof, for these methods would have straightway led him to a conclusion exactly opposite to the one he wished to establish. So he turned to dialectical speculation, which was, moreover, in keeping with the bent of his mind. And here it was a case of help what can. He knew the result that he wished to obtain, and must obtain, and so he twisted and manipulated the patient ideas and logical premises with admirable skill and subtlety until they actually yielded the desired result in a seemingly respectable syllogistic form. Perhaps he was so blinded by his convictions that he was not aware of the monstrosities of logic and method which had necessarily crept in, or perhaps he was aware of them and thought himself justified in making use of them simply as formal supports, to give a suitable systematic dress to a truth which, according to his deepest convictions, was already substantially proved. Of that I cannot judge, neither is it now possible for any one else to do so. What I will say, however, is that no one, with so powerful a mind as Marx, has ever exhibited a logic so continuously and so palpably wrong as he exhibits in the systematic proof of his fundamental doctrine.

Section Two

This wrong thesis he now weaves into his system with admirable tactical skill. Of this we have a brilliant example in the next step he takes. Although he has carefully steered clear of the testimony of experience and has evolved his doctrine entirely "out of the depths of his mind," yet the wish to apply the test of experience cannot be altogether suppressed. If Marx himself would not do it, his readers would certainly do it on their own account. What does he do? He divides and distinguishes. At one point the disagreement between his doctrine and experience is flagrant. Taking the bull by the horns he himself seizes upon this point. He had stated as a consequence of his fundamental principle that the value of different commodities is in proportion to the working time necessary to their production (i. 14). Now it is obvious even to the casual observer that this proposition cannot maintain itself in the face of certain facts. The day's product of a sculptor, of a cabinet-maker, of a violin maker, of an engineer, &c., certainly does not contain an equal value, but a much higher value than the day's product of a common workman or factory hand, although in both the same amount of working time is "embodied." Marx himself, with a masterly dialectic, now brings these facts up for discussion. In considering them he seeks to suggest that they do not contain a contradiction of his fundamental principle, but are only a slightly different reading of it which still comes within the limits of the rule, and that all that is needed is some explanation or more exact definition of the latter. That is to say he declares that labour in the sense of his proposition means the "expenditure of simple [unskilled] working power, an average of which is possessed in his physical organism by every ordinary man, without special cultivation"; or in other words *"simple average labour"* (i. 19, and also previously in i.13).

"Skilled labour," he continues, *"counts only as concentrated or rather multiplied unskilled labour,* so that a small quantity of skilled labour is equal to a larger quantity of unskilled labour. *That this reduction is constantly made experience shows.* A commodity may be the product of the most highly skilled labour, but *its value makes it equal to the product of unskilled labour, and represents therefore only a definite quantity of unskilled labour.* The different proportions in which different kinds of labour are reduced to unskilled labour as their unit of measure are fixed by a social process beyond the control of the producers, and therefore seem given to them by tradition."

This explanation may really sound quite plausible to the hasty reader, but if we look at it coolly and soberly we get quite a different impression.

The fact with which we have to deal is that the product of a day's or an hour's skilled labour is more valuable than the product of a day's or an hour's unskilled labour; that, for instance, the day's product of a sculptor is equal to the five days' product of a stone-breaker. Now Marx tells us that things made equal to each other in exchange must contain "a common factor of the same amount," and this common factor must be labour and working time. Does he mean labour in general? Marx's first statements up to page 13 would lead us to suppose so; but it is evident that something is wrong, for the labour of five days is obviously not "the same amount" as the labour of one day. Therefore Marx, in the case before us, is no longer speaking of labour as such but of unskilled labour. The common factor must therefore be the possession of an equal amount of labour of a particular kind, viz., unskilled labour.

If we look at this dispassionately, however, it fits still worse, for in sculpture there is no "unskilled labour" at all embodied, much less therefore unskilled labour equal to the amount in the five days' labour of the stone-breaker. The plain truth is that the two products embody *different kinds* of labour in *different amounts,* and every unprejudiced person will admit that this means a state of things exactly contrary to the conditions which Marx demands and must affirm, viz., that they embody labour of the *same kind* and of the *same amount!*

Marx certainly says that skilled labour "counts" as multiplied unskilled labour, but to "count as" is not "to be," and the theory deals with the being of things. Men may naturally consider one day of a sculptor's work as equal in some respects to five days of a stone-breaker's work, just as they may also consider a deer as equal to five hares. But a statistician might with equal justification maintain, with scientific conviction, that there were one thousand hares in a cover which contained one hundred deer and five hundred hares, as a statistician of prices or a theorist about value might seriously maintain that in the day's product of a sculptor five days of unskilled labour are embodied, and that this is the true reason why it is considered in exchange to be equal to five days' labour of a stone-breaker. I will presently attempt to illustrate, by an example bearing directly on the problem of value, the multitude of things we might prove if we resorted to the verb "to count" whenever the verb " to be," &c., landed us in difficulties. But I must first add one other criticism.

Marx makes an attempt in the passages quoted to justify his manoeuvre of reducing skilled labour to common labour, and to justify it by experience.

"That this reduction is constantly made experience shows. A commodity may be the product of the most highly skilled labour, but its value makes it equal to the product of unskilled labour, and represents therefore only a definite quantity of unskilled labour."

Good! We will let that pass for the moment and will only inquire a little more closely in what manner and by what means we are to determine the standard of this reduction, which, according to Marx, experience shows is constantly made. Here we stumble against the very natural, but for the Marxian theory the very compromising circumstance that the standard of reduction is determined solely *by the actual exchange relations themselves.* But in what proportions skilled is to be translated into terms of simple labour in the valuation of their products is not determined, nor can it be determined *a priori* by any property inherent in the skilled labour itself, but it is the actual result alone which decides the actual exchange relations. Marx himself says "their value makes them equal to the product of unskilled labour," and he refers to a "social process beyond the control of the producers which fixes the proportions in which different kinds of labour are reduced to unskilled labour as their unit of measure," and says that these proportions therefore *"seem to be given by tradition."*

Under these circumstances what is the meaning of the appeal to "value" and "the social process" as the determining factors of the standard of reduction Apart from everything else it simply means that Marx is arguing in a complete circle. The real subject of inquiry is the exchange relations of commodities: why, for instance, a statuette which has cost a sculptor one day's labour should exchange for a cart of stones which has cost a stone breaker five days' labour, and not for a larger or smaller quantity of stones, in the breaking of which ten or three days' labour have been expended. How does Marx explain this? He says the exchange relation is this, and no other–because one day of sculptor's work is reducible exactly to five days of unskilled work. And why is it reducible to exactly five days? Because experience shows that it is so reduced by a social process. And what is this social process? The same process that has to be explained, that very process by means of which the product of one day of sculptor's labour has been made equal to the value of the product of five days of common labour. But if as a matter of fact it were exchanged regularly against the product of only three days of simple labour, Marx would equally bid us accept the rate of reduction of 1:3 as the one derived from experience, and would found upon it and explain by it the assertion that a statuette must be equal in exchange to the product of exactly three days of a stone-breaker's work–not more and not less. In short, it is clear that we shall never learn in this way the actual reasons why products of different kinds of work should be exchanged in this or that proportion. They exchange in this way, Marx tells us, though in slightly different words, because, according to experience, they do exchange in this way!

I remark further in passing that the successors *(epigoni)* of Marx, having perhaps recognised the circle I have just described, have made the attempt to place the reduction of complicated to simple work on another, a real, basis.

"It is no fiction but a fact," says Grabski, [6] "that an hour of skilled labour contains several hours of unskilled labour." For "in order to be consistent, we must also take into account the labour which was used in acquiring the skill." I do not think it will need many words to show clearly the complete inadequacy also of this explanation. I have nothing to say against the view that to labour in actual operation should be added the quota due to the acquirement of the power to labour. But it is clear that the difference in value of skilled labour as opposed to unskilled labour could only then be explained by reference to this additional quota if the amount of the latter corresponded to the amount of that difference. For instance, in the case we have given, there could only be actually five hours of unskilled labour in one hour of skilled labour, if four hours of preparatory labour went to every hour of skilled labour; or, reckoned in greater units, if out of fifty years of life which a sculptor devotes to the learning and practising of his profession, he spends forty years in educational work in order to do skilled work for tell years. But no one will maintain that such a proportion or anything approaching to it is actually found to exist. I turn therefore again from the obviously inadequate hypothesis of the successor *(epigonos)* to the teaching of the master himself in order to illustrate the nature and range of its errors by one other example, which I think will bring out most clearly the fault in Marx's mode of reasoning.

With the very same reasoning one could affirm and argue the proposition that the quantity of material contained in commodities constitutes the principle and measure of exchange value—that commodities exchange in proportion to the *quantity of material incorporated in them.* Ten lbs. of material in one kind of commodity exchange against to lbs. of material in another kind of commodity. If the natural objection were raised that this statement was obviously false because 10 lbs. of gold do not exchange against 10 lbs. of iron but against 40,000 lbs., or against a still greater number of pounds of coal, we may reply after the manner of Marx, that it is the amount of *common average material* that affects the formation of value, that acts as unit of measurement. Skillfully wrought costly material of special quality *counts* only as compound or rather multiplied common material, so that a small quantity of material fashioned with skill is equal to a larger quantity of common material. *That this reduction is constantly made experience shows.* A commodity may be of the most exquisite material; its *value* makes it equal to commodities formed of common material, and *therefore represents only a particular quantity of common material.* A "social process," the existence of which cannot be doubted, is persistently reducing the pound of raw gold to 40,000 lbs. of raw iron, and the pound of raw silver to 1,500 lbs. of raw iron. The working up of the gold by an ordinary goldsmith or by the hand of a great artist gives rise to further variations in the character of the material to which use, in conformity with experience, does justice by means of special standards of reduction. If I lb. of bar gold, therefore, exchanges against 40,000 lbs. of bar iron, or if a gold cup of the same weight, wrought by Benvenuto Cellini, exchanges against 4,000,000 lbs. of iron, it is not a violation but a confirmation of the proposition that commodities exchange in proportion to the "average" material they contain!

I think the impartial reader will easily recognise once more in these two arguments the two ingredients of the Marxian receipt—the substitution of "to count" for "to be," and the explanation in a circle which consists in obtaining the standard of reduction from the actually existing social exchange relations which themselves need explanation. In this way Marx has settled his account with the facts that most glaringly contradict his theory with great dialectical skill, certainly, but, as far as the matter itself is concerned, naturally and inevitably in a quite inadequate manner.

But there are, besides, contradictions with actual experience rather less striking than the foregoing; those, namely, which spring from the part that the *investment of capital* has in determining the actual prices of commodities, the same which Ricardo–as we have already noticed–treats of in Section IV. of the chapter "On Value." Towards them Marx adopts a change of tactics. For a time he completely shuts his eyes to them. He ignores them, by a process of abstraction, through the first and second volumes, and pretends that they do not exist; that is to say, he proceeds throughout the whole detailed exposition of his doctrine of value, and likewise throughout the development of his theory of surplus value, on the "assumption"–in part tacitly maintained, in part clearly asserted–that commodities really exchange according to their values, which means exactly in proportion to the labour embodied in them. [7]

This hypothetical abstraction he combines with an uncommonly clever dialectical move. He gives certain actual deviations from the law, from which a theorist may really venture to abstract, namely, the accidental and temporary fluctuations of the market prices round their normal fixed level. And on the occasions when Marx explains his intention to disregard the deviations of the prices from the values he does not fail to direct the reader's attention to those "accidental circumstances" which have to be ignored as "the constant oscillations of the market prices," whose "rise and fall compensate each other," and which "reduce themselves to an average price as their inner law." [8] By this reference he gains the reader's approval of his abstraction, but the fact that he does not abstract merely from accidental fluctuations but also from regular, permanent, typical "deviations," whose existence constitutes an integral part of the rule to be elucidated, is not made manifest to the reader who is not closely observant, and he glides unsuspectingly over the author's fatal error of method.

For it is a fatal error of method to ignore in scientific investigation the very point that demands explanation. Now Marx's theory of surplus value aims at nothing else than the explanation, as he conceives it, of the profits of capital. But the profits of capital lie exactly in those regular deviations of the prices of commodities from the amount of their mere costs in labour. If, therefore, we ignore those deviations, we ignore just the principal part of what has to be explained. Rodbertus [9] was guilty of the same error of method, and twelve years ago I taxed him, as well as Marx, with it; and I venture now to repeat the concluding words of the criticism I then made:–

"They (the adherents of the exploitation theory) maintain the law that the value of all commodities rests on the working time embodied in them in order that the next moment they may attack as "opposed to law," "unnatural"

55

and "unjust," all forms of value that do not harmonise with this "law" (such as the difference in value that falls as surplus to the capitalist), and demand their abolition. Thus they first ignore the exceptions in order to proclaim their law of value as universal. And after thus assuming its universality they again draw attention to the exceptions in order to brand them as offences against the law. This kind of argument is very much as if we were to assume that there were many foolish people in the world, and to ignore that there were also many wise ones, and then, coming to the "universally valid law" that "all men are foolish," should demand the extirpation of the wise on the ground that their existence is obviously "contrary to law." [10]

By his manoeuvre of abstraction Marx certainly gained a great tactical advantage for his own version of the case. He, "by hypothesis," shut out from his system the disturbing real world, and did not therefore, so long as he could maintain this exclusion, come into conflict with it; and he does maintain it through the greater part of the first volume, through the whole of the second volume, and through the first quarter of the third volume. In this middle part of the Marxian system the logical development and connection present a really imposing closeness and intrinsic consistency. Marx is free to use good logic here because, by means of hypothesis, he has in advance made the facts to square with his ideas, and call therefore be true to the latter without knocking up against the former. And when Marx is free to use sound logic he does so in a truly masterly way. However wrong the starting point may be, these middle parts of the system, by their extraordinary logical consistency, permanently establish the reputation of the author as an intellectual force of the first rank. And it is a circumstance that has served not a little to increase the practical influence of the Marxian system that during this long middle part of his work, which, as far as intrinsic consistency is concerned, is really essentially faultless, the readers who have got happily over the difficulties at the beginning get time to accustom themselves to the Marxian world of thought and to gain confidence in his connection of ideas, which here how so smoothly, one out of the other, and form themselves into such a well-arranged whole. it is on these readers, whose confidence has been thus won, that he makes those hard demands which he is at last obliged to bring forward in his third volume. For, long as Marx delayed to open his eyes to the facts of real life, he had to do it some time or other. He had at last to confess to his readers that in actual life commodities do not exchange, regularly and of necessity, in proportion to the working time incorporated in them, but in part exchange above and in part below this proportion, according as the capital invested demands a smaller or a larger amount of the average profit; in short that, besides working time, investment of capital forms a co-ordinate determinant of the exchange relation of commodities. From this point he was confronted with two difficult tasks. In the first place he had to justify himself to his readers for having in the earlier parts of his work and for so long taught that labour was the sole determinant of exchange relations; and secondly–what was perhaps the more difficult task–he had also to give his readers a theoretical explanation of the facts which were hostile to his theory, an explanation which certainly could trot fit into his labour theory of value without leaving a residuum, but which must not, on the other hand, contradict it.

One can understand that good straightforward logic could no longer be used in these demonstrations. We now witness the counterpart to the confused beginning of the system. There Marx had to do violence to facts in order to deduce a theorem which could not be straightforwardly deduced from them, and he had to do still greater violence to logic and commit the most incredible fallacies into the bargain. Now the situation repeats itself. Now again the propositions which through two volumes have been in undisturbed possession of the field come into collision with the facts with which they are naturally as little in agreement as they were before. Nevertheless the harmony of the system has to be maintained, and it can only be maintained at the cost of the logic. The Marxian system, therefore, presents us now with a spectacle at first sight strange, but, under the circumstances described, quite natural, viz., that by far the greater part of the system is a masterpiece of close and forcible logic worthy of the intellect of its author, but that in two places–and those, alas! just the most decisive places–incredibly weak and careless reasoning is inserted. The first place is just at the beginning when the theory first separates itself from the facts, and the second is after the first quarter of the third volume when facts are again brought within the horizon of the reader. I here refer more especially to the tenth chapter of the third book (pp. 151-79).

We have already become acquainted with one part of its contents, and we have subjected it to our criticism, the part, namely, where Marx defends himself against the accusation that there is a contradiction between the law of the price of production and the "law of value." [11] It still remains, however, to glance at the second object with which the chapter is concerned, the explanation with which Marx introduces into his system that theory of the price of production which takes account of actual conditions. [12] This consideration leads us also to one of the most instructive and most characteristic points of the Marxian system–the points of "competition" in the system.

Section Three

"Competition," as I have already hinted, is a sort of collective name for all the psychical motives and impulses which determine the action of the dealers in the market, and which thus influence the fixing of prices. The buyer has his motives which actuate him in buying, and which provide him with a certain guide as to the prices which he is prepared to offer either at once or in the last resort. And the seller and the producer are also actuated by certain motives–motives which determine the seller to part with his commodities at a certain price and not at another price, and the producer to continue and even to extend his production when prices reach a certain level, or to suspend it when they are at a different level. In the competition between buyer and seller all these motives and determinants encounter each other, and whoever refers to competition to explain the formation of prices appeals in effect to what under a collective name is the active play of all the psychical impulses and motives which had directed both sides of the market.

Marx is now, for the most part, engaged in the endeavour to give to competition and the forces operating in it the lowest possible place in his system. He either ignores it, or, if he does not do this, he tries to belittle the manner and degree of its influence where and whenever he can. This is shown in a striking way on several occasions.

First of all he does this when he deduces his law that value is wholly labour. Every impartial person knows and sees that influence which the quantity of labour employed exerts on the permanent level of prices of goods (an influence not really so special and peculiar as the Marxian law of value makes it appear) acts only through the play of supply and demand, that is to say, through competition. In the case of exceptional exchanges, or in the case of monopoly, prices may come into existence which (even apart from the claim of the capital invested) are out of all proportion to the working time incorporated. Marx naturally knows this too, but he makes no reference to it in his deduction of the law of value. If he had referred to it, then he would have been unable to put aside the question in what way and by what middle steps working time should come to be the sole influence determining the level price among all the motives and factors which play their part under the flag of competition. The complete analysis of those motives, which then could not have been avoided, would inevitably have placed the value in use much more in the foreground than would have suited Marx, and would have cast a different light on many things, and finally would have revealed much to which Marx did not wish to allow any weight in his system.

And so on the very occasion when, in order to give a complete and systematic explanation of his law of value, it would have been his duty to have shown the part which competition plays as intermediary, he passes away from the point without a word. Later on he does notice it, but, to judge from the place and the manner, not as if it were an important point in the theoretic system; in some casual and cursory remarks he alludes to it in a few words as something that more or less explains itself, and he does not trouble himself to go further into it.

I think that the said facts about competition are most clearly and concisely set forth by Marx in page 156 of the third volume, where the exchange of commodities at prices which approximate to their "values" and correspond therefore to the working time incorporated in them is said to be subject to the three following conditions: I. That the exchange of commodities be not merely an *"accidental or occasional one."* 2. That commodities "on both sides should be produced in quantities nearly proportionate to the reciprocal demand, *which itself results from the experience of both sides of the market, and which therefore grows as a result out of a sustained exchange itself;"* and 3.

58

"That no natural or artificial monopoly should give to either of the contract-ing parties the power to sell above the value, or should force either of them to sell below the value." And so what Marx demands as a condition of his law of value coming into operation is a brisk competition on both sides which should have lasted long enough to adjust production relatively to the needs of the buyer according to the experience of the market. We must bear this passage well in mind.

No more detailed proof is added. On the contrary, a little later–indeed, just in the middle of those arguments in which, relatively speaking, he treats moat exhaustively of competition, its two sides of demand and supply, and its relation to the fixing of prices-Marx expressly declines a "deeper analysis of these two social impelling forces" as "not apposite here." [13]

But this is not all. In order to belittle the importance, for the theoretic sys-tem, of supply and demand, and perhaps also to justify his neglect of these factors, Marx thought out a peculiar and remarkable theory which he devel-ops on pages 169-70 of the third volume, after some previous slight allusions to it. He starts by saying that when one of the two factors preponderates over the other, demand over supply, for instance, or *vice versa,* irregular market prices are formed which deviate from the "market value," which constitutes the "point of equilibrium" for these market prices; that, on the other hand, if commodities should sell at this their normal market value, demand and sup-ply must exactly balance each other. And to that he adds the following re-markable argument: "If demand and supply balance each other *they cease to act.* If two forces act equally in opposite directions they cancel each other–they produce no result, and phenomena occurring under these conditions *must be explained by some other agency than either of these forces.* If supply and demand cancel each other *they cease to explain anything, they do not af-fect the market value,* and they leave us altogether in the dark as to the rea-sons why the market value should express itself in just this and no other "sum of money." The relation of demand to supply can be rightly used to ex-plain the "deviations from the market value" which are due to the prepon-derance of one force over the other, but not the level of the market value it-self.

That this curious theory squared with the Marxian system is obvious. If the relation of supply to demand had absolutely no bearing on the level of per-manent prices, then Marx was quite right, in laying down his principles, not to trouble himself further with this unimportant factor, and straightway to introduce into his system the factor which, in his opinion, exercised a real influence on the degree of value, that is, labour.

It is, however, not less obvious, I think, that this curious theory is absolute-ly false. Its reasoning rests, as is so often the case with Marx, on a play upon words.

It is quite true that when a commodity sells at its normal market value, supply and demand must in a certain sense balance each other: that is to say, at this price, just the same quantity of the commodity is effectively demanded as is offered. But this is not only the case when commodities are sold at a normal market value, but at whatever market value they are sold, even when it is a varying irregular one. Moreover, every one knows quite well, as does Marx himself, that supply and demand are elastic quantities. In addition to the supply and demand which enters into exchange, there is always an "excluded " demand or supply, i.e., a number of people who equally desire the commodities for their needs, but who will not or cannot offer the prices offered by their stronger competitors; and a number of people who are also prepared to offer the desired commodities, only at higher prices than can be obtained in the then state of the market. But the saying that demand and supply "balance each other" does not apply absolutely to the *total* demand and supply, but only to the *successful part of it.* It is well known, however, that the business of the market consists just in selecting the successful part out of the total demand and the total supply, and that the most important means to this selection is the fixing of price. More commodities cannot be bought than are sold. Hence, on the two sides, only a certain fixed number of reflectors (i.e., reflectors for only a certain fixed number of commodities) call arrive at a focus. The selection of this number is accomplished by the automatic advance of prices to a point which excludes the excess in number on both sides; so that the price is at the same time too high for the excess of the would-be buyers and too low for the excess of the would-be sellers. It is not, therefore, the successful competitors only who take part in determining the level of prices, but the respective circumstances of those who are excluded have a share in it as well; [14] and on that account, if on no other, it is wrong to argue the complete suspension of the action of supply and demand from the equilibrium of the part which comes effectively into the market.

But it is wrong also for another reason. Assuming that it is only the successful part of supply and demand, being in quantitative equilibrium, that affects the fixing of price, it is quite erroneous and unscientific to assume that forces which hold each other in equilibrium therefore " cease to act." On the contrary, the state of equilibrium is just the result of their action, and when an explanation has to be given of this state of equilibrium with all its details–one of the most prominent of which is the height of the level in which the equilibrium was found–it certainly cannot be given "in some other way than by the agency of the two forces." On the contrary, it is only by the agency of the forces which maintain the equilibrium that it can be explained· But such abstract propositions can best be illustrated by a practical example.

Suppose we send up an air-balloon. Everybody knows that a balloon rises if and because it is filled with a gas which is thinner than the atmospheric air. It does not rise into the illimitable, however, but only to a certain height, where it remains floating so long as nothing occurs, such as an escape of gas, to alter the conditions. Now how is the degree of altitude regulated, and by what factor is it determined? This is transparently evident. The density of atmospheric air diminishes as we rise. The balloon rises only so long as the density of the surrounding stratum of atmosphere is greater than its own density, and it ceases to rise when its own density and the density; of the atmosphere hold each other in equipoise. The less dense the gas, therefore, the higher the balloon will rise, and the higher the stratum of air in which it finds the same degree of atmospheric density. It is obvious, under these circumstances, therefore, that the height to which the balloon rises cannot be explained considering the relative density of the on one side and of the atmospheric air other.

How does the matter appear, however, from the Marxian point of view? At a certain height both forces, density of the balloon and density of the surrounding air, are in equipoise. They, therefore, "cease to act," "they cease to explain anything," they do not affect the degree of, ascent, and if we wish to explain this we must do it by "something else than the agency of these two forces." Indeed, we say, By what then? Or again, when the index of a weighing machine points to 100 lbs. when a body is being weighed, how are we to account for this position of the index of the weighing machine? We are *not* to account for it by the relation of the weight of the body to be weighed on the one side and the weights which serve in the weighing machine on the other, for these two forces, when the index of the weighing machine is in the position referred to, hold each other in equipoise; they therefore cease to act, and nothing can be explained from their relationship, not even the position of the index of the weighing machine.

I think the fallacy here is obvious, and that it is not less obvious that the same kind of fallacy lies at the root of the arguments by which Marx reasons away the influence of supply and demand on the level of permanent prices. Let there be no misunderstanding, however. It is by no means my opinion that a really complete and satisfying explanation of the fixing of permanent prices is contained in a reference to the formula of supply and demand. On the contrary, the opinion, which I have elsewhere often expressed at length, is that the elements which can only be roughly comprehended under the term "supply and demand" ought to be closely analysed, and the manner and measure of their reciprocal influence exactly defined; and that in this way we should proceed to the attainment of the knowledge of those elements which exert a special influence on the state of prices. But the influence of the relation of supply and demand which Marx reasons away is an indispensable link in this further and more profound explanation; it is not a side issue, but one that goes to the heart of the subject.

Let us take up again the threads of our argument. Various things have shown us how hard Marx tries to make the influence of supply and demand retire into the background of his system, and now at the remarkable turn which his system takes after the first quarter of the third volume he is confronted by the task of explaining why the permanent prices of commodities do not gravitate towards the incorporated quantity of labour but towards the "prices of production" which deviate from it.

He declares competition to be which causes this. Competition reduces the original rates of profit, which were different for the different branches of production according to the different organic compositions of the capitals, to a common average rate of profit, [15] and consequently the prices must in the long run gravitate towards the prices of production yielding the one equal average profit.

Let us hasten to settle some points which are important to the understanding of this explanation.

Firstly, it is certain that a reference to competition is in effect nothing else than a reference to the action of supply and demand. In the passage already mentioned, in which Marx describes most concisely the process of the equalisation of the rates of profit by the competition of capitals (iii.175), he expressly says that this process is brought about by "such a relation of supply to demand, that the average profit is made equal in the different spheres of production, and that therefore values change into prices of production."

Secondly, it is certain that, as regards this process, it is not a question of mere *fluctuations* round the centre of gravitation contemplated in the theory of the first two volumes, i.e., round the incorporated working time, but a question of a *definitive forcing* of prices to another permanent centre of gravitation, viz., the price of production.

And now question follows on question.

If, according to Marx, the relation of supply and demand exerts no influence at all on the level of permanent prices, how can competition, which is identical with this relation, be the power which shifts the level of the permanent prices from the level of "value" to a level so different as that of the price of production?

Do we not rather see, in this forced and inconsistent appeal to competition as the *deus ex machina* which drives the permanent prices from that centre of gravitation which is in keeping with the theory of embodied labour to another centre, an involuntary confession that the social forces which govern actual life contain in themselves, and bring into action, some elementary determinants of exchange relations which *cannot* be reduced to working time, and that consequently the analysis of the original theory which yielded working time alone as the basis of exchange relations was an incomplete one which did not correspond with the facts?

And further: Marx has told us himself, and we have carefully noted the passage, [16] that commodities exchange approximately to their values only when a brisk competition exists. Thus he, at that time, appealed to competition as a factor which tends to push the prices of commodities towards their " values." And now we learn, on the contrary, that competition is a force which pushes the prices of commodities away from their values and on to their prices of production. These statements, moreover, are found in one and the same chapter–the tenth chapter, destined, it would seem, to an unhappy notoriety. Can they be reconciled? And, if Marx perhaps thought that he could find a reconciliation in the view that one proposition applied to primitive conditions and the other to developed modern society, must we not point out to him that in the first chapter of his work he did not deduce his theory that value was wholly labour from a *Robinsonade,* but from the conditions of a society in which a "capitalistic mode of production prevails" and the "'wealth " of which "appears as an immense collection of commodities"? And does he not demand of us throughout his whole work that we should view the conditions of our modern society in the light of his theory of labour, and judge them by it? But when we ask where, according to his own statements, we are to seek in modern society for the region in which his law of value is in force, we ask in vain. For either there is no competition, in which case commodities do not at all exchange according to their values, says Marx (iii. 156); or competition exists, and precisely then, he states, they still less exchange according to their values, but according to their prices of production (iii. 176).

And so in the unfortunate tenth chapter contradiction is heaped upon contradiction. I will not prolong the already lengthy inquiry by counting up all the lesser contradictions and inaccuracies with which this chapter abounds. I think every one who reads the chapter with an impartial mind will get the impression that the writing is, so to say, demoralised. Instead of the severe, pregnant, careful style, instead of the iron logic to which we are accustomed in the most brilliant parts of Marx's works, we have here an uncertain and desultory manner not only in the reasoning but even in the use of technical terms. How striking, for instance, is the constantly changing conception of the terms "supply" and "demand," which at one time are presented to us, quite rightly, as elastic quantities, with differences of intensity, but at another are regarded, after the worst manner of a long-exploded "vulgar economy," as simple quantities. Or how unsatisfying and inconsistent is the description of the factors which govern the market value, if the different portions of the mass of commodities which come into the market are created under unequal conditions of production, &c.

The explanation of this feature of the chapter cannot be found simply in the fact that it was written by Marx when he was growing old; for even in later parts there are many splendidly written arguments; and even this unfortunate chapter, of which obscure hints were already scattered here and there in the first volume, [17] must have been *through out* in early times. Marx's writing is confused and vacillating here because he could not venture to write clearly and definitely without open contradiction and retractation. If at the time when he was dealing with actual exchange relations–those manifested in real life–he had pursued the subject with the same luminous penetration and thoroughness with which he followed, through two volumes, the hypothesis that value is labour to its utmost logical conclusion ; if at this juncture he had given to the important term "competition" a scientific import, by a careful economico-psychological analysis of the social motive forces which come into. action under that comprehensive name; if he had not halted or rested, so long as a link in the argument remained unexplained, or a consequence not carried to its logical conclusion; or so long as one relation appeared dark and contradictory–and almost every word of this tenth chapter challenges a deeper inquiry or explanation such as this–he would have been driven step by step to the exposition of a system altogether different in purport from that of his original system, nor would he have been able to avoid the open contradiction and retractation of the main proposition of the original system. This could only be avoided by confusion and mystification. Marx must often instinctively have felt this, even if he did not know it, when he expressly declined the deeper analysis of the social motive forces.

Herein lies, I believe, the Alpha and Omega of all that is fallacious, contradictory, and vague in the treatment of his subject by Marx. His system is not in close touch with facts. Marx has not deduced from facts the fundamental principles of his system, either by means of a sound empiricism or a solid economico-psychological analysis; but he founds it on no firmer ground than a formal dialectic. This is the great radical fault of the Marxian system at its birth; from it all the rest necessarily springs. The system runs in one direction, facts go in another; and they cross the course of the system sometimes here, sometimes there, and on each occasion the original fault begets a new fault. The conflict of system and facts must be kept from view, so that the matter is shrouded either in darkness or vagueness, or it is turned and twisted with the same tricks of dialectic as at the outset; or where none of this avails we have a contradiction. Such is the character of the tenth chapter of Marx's third volume. It brings the long-deferred bad harvest, which grew by necessity out of the bad seed.

[1] *Geschichte und Kritik der Kapitalzinstheorieen,* pp. 429 seq. Engl. Transl., p. 377.

[2] Karl Knies makes the following pertinent objection against Marx: "There is no reason apparent in Marx's statement why the equation, 1 quarter wheat = a cwts. wild grown wood = b acres of virgin soil = c acres of natural pasture-land, should not be as good as the equation, 1 quarter wheat = a cwts. of forest-sown wood" *(Das Geld,* 1st edition, p. 121, 2nd edition, p. 157).

[3] In a quotation from Barbon, in this same paragraph, the difference between commodities and things is again effaced: " One sort of *wares* are as good as another, if the value be equal. There is no difference or distinction in things of equal *value.*"

[4] For example, p. 15, at end: "Lastly, nothing can be a value without also being an object of use. If it is useless, the labour contained in it is also useless; it does not count as labour (sic!), and therefore creates no value." Knies has already drawn attention to the logical fallacy animadverted upon in the text. (See *Das Geld,* Berlin, 1873, pp. 123 seq.; 2nd edition, pp. 160 seq.) Adler *(Grundlagen der Karl Marxchen Kritik,* Tubingen, 1887, pp. 211 seq.) has strangely misunderstood my argument when he contends against me that good voices are not commodities in the Marxian sense. It did not concern me at all whether "good voices" could be classed as economic goods under the Marxian law of value or not. It only concerned me to present an argument of a logical syllogism which showed the same fallacy as that of Marx. I might for this purpose just as well have chosen an example which was in no way related to the domain of economics. I might, for example, just as well have shown that according to Marx's logic the common fac-

tor of *variously coloured* bodies might consist in heaven knows what, but not in the blending of various colours. For any one combination of colours–for example, white, blue, yellow, black, violet–is as regards variety worth just as much as any other combination, say green, red, orange, sky-blue, &c., if only it is present "in proper proportion"; we therefore apparently abstract from the colour and combination of colours!

[5] The position which is taken by Smith and Ricardo towards the doctrine that value is wholly labour i have discussed exhaustively in the *Geschichte und Kritik*, pp. 428 seq., and have there also shown especially that no trace of a proof of this thesis is to be found in the so-called classical writers. Compare also Knies, *Der Kredit*, 2nd section, pp. 60 seq.

[6] *Deutsche Worte*, vol, xv., part 3, March, 1895, p. 155.

[7] For example, 141 seq., 150, 151, 158, and often; also in the beginning of the third vol., iii. 25, 128, 132.

[8] For example, i. 150, note 37.

[9] As to Rodbertus, see the exhaustive account in my *Geschichte und Kritik*, pp. 405 seq., more especially the note on p. 407; translation, pp. 359 seq., 356 note.

[10] Ibid., pp. 443 seq.; transl., p. 388.

[11] See above.

[12] Of course I here quite disregard comparatively small differences of opinion. I have especially refrained in the whole of this paragraph from emphasising or even mentioning the finer shades of difference which obtain in relation to the conception of the "law of costs."

[13] III. 169. See also above.

[14] A closer analysis shows that the price must fall between the money estimates of the so-called marginal pairs, that is, between the amounts which the last actual buyer and the first would-be buyer who is excluded from the market are prepared to offer, and the amounts which the last actual seller and the first would-be seller who is excluded are prepared to take in the last resort for the commodities. For further details see my *Positive Theorie des Kapitals*, Innsbruck, 1889, pp. 218 seq.; English translation by Prof. Smart (Macmillan, 1891), p. 208.

[15] See above.

[16] See above, pp. 175-6 seq.

[17] For example, i. p. 151, note 37 at foot; p. 210, note 31.

Chapter Five - Werner Sombart's Apology

AN apologist of Marx, as intelligent as he is ardent, has lately appeared in the person of Werner Sombart. [1] His apology, however, shows one peculiar feature. In order to be able to defend Marx's doctrines he has first to put a new interpretation upon them.

Let us go at once to the main point. Sombart admits (and even adds some very subtle arguments to the proof) [2] that the Marxian law of value is false if it claims to be in harmony with actual experience. He says (p. 573) Of the

Marxian law of value that it " is not exhibited in the exchange relation of capitalistically produced commodities," that it "does not by any means indicate the point towards which market prices gravitate," that *just as little* does it act as a factor of distribution in the division of the social yearly product," and that "it *never comes into evidence anywhere*" (p. 577). The "outlawed value" has only "one place of refuge left–*the thought of the theoretical economist.....* If we want to sum up the characteristics of Marx's value, we would say, *his value is fact not of experience but of thought*" (p. 574).

What Sombart means by this "existence in thought" we shall see directly; but first we must stop for a moment to consider the admission that the Marxian value has no existence in the world of real phenomena. I am somewhat curious to know whether the Marxists will ratify this admission. It may well be doubted, as Sombart himself had to quote a protest from the Marxian camp, occasioned by an utterance of C. Schmidt and raised in advance against such a view. "The law of value is not a law of our thought merely; ... the law of value is a law of a very real nature: it is a natural law of human action." [3] I think it also very questionable whether Marx himself would have ratified the admission. It is Sombart himself who again, with noteworthy frankness, gives the reader a whole list of passages from Marx which make this interpretation difficult. [4] For my own part I hold it to be wholly irreconcilable with the letter and spirit of the Marxian teaching. Let any one read without bias the arguments with which Marx develops his value of theory. He begins his inquiry, as he himself says, in the domain of "capitalistically organised society, whose wealth is an immense collection of commodities," and with the analysis of a commodity (i. 9). In order to "get on the track" of value he starts from the exchange relation of the commodity (i. 23). Does he start from an actual exchange relation, I ask, or from an imaginary one? If he had said or meant the latter, no reader would have thought it worth while to pursue so idle a speculation. He does indeed make very decided reference–as was inevitable–to the phenomena of the actual economic world. The exchange relation of two commodities, he says, can always be represented by an equation: thus 1 quarter wheat = 1 cwt. iron. "What does this equation prove? *That a common factor of the same magnitude exists* in both things, and each of the two, *in so far as it is an exchange value, must be reducible* to this third," which third, as we learn on the next page, is labour of the same quantity.

If you maintain that the same quantity of labour exists in things made equal in exchange, and that these things must be reducible to equal amounts of labour, you are claiming for these conditions an existence in the real world and not merely in thought. Marx's former line of argument, we must bear in mind, would have been quite impossible if by the side of it he had wished to propound, for actual exchange relations, the dogma that products of unequal amounts of labour exchange, on principle, with each other. If he had admitted this notion (and the conflict with facts with which I reproach him lies just in his not admitting it), he would certainly have come to quite different conclusions. Either he would have been obliged to declare that the so-called equalisation in exchange is no true equation, and does not admit of the conclusion that "a common factor *of equal magnitude*" is present in the exchanged things, or he would have been obliged to come to the conclusion that the sought-for common factor of equal magnitude is *not,* and could not be *labour.* In any case it would have been impossible for him to have continued to reason as he did.

And Marx goes on to say very decidedly on numerous occasions that his "value" lies at the root of exchange relations, so that indeed products of equal amount of labour are " equivalents," and as such exchange for each other. [5] In many places, some of which are quoted by Sombart himself, [6] he claims that his law of value possesses the character and the potency of a *law of nature,* "it forces its way as the law of gravity does when the house comes down over one's head." [7] Even in the third volume he distinctly sets forth the actual conditions (they amount to a brisk competition on both sides) which must obtain "in order that the prices at which commodities exchange with each other should correspond approximately to their value," and explains further that this " naturally only signifies that their value is the centre of gravitation round which their prices move" (iii. 156).

We may mention in this connection that Marx also often quotes with approval older writers who maintained the proposition that the exchange value of goods was determined by the labour embodied in them, and maintained it undoubtedly as a proposition which was in harmony with actual exchange relations. [8] Sombart himself, moreover, notes an argument of Marx's in which he quite distinctly claims for his law of value an "empirical " and "historical" truth (iii. 155 in connection with iii. 175 seq.).

And finally, if Marx claimed only a validity in thought and not in things for his law of value, what meaning would there have been in the painful efforts we have described, with which he sought to prove that, in spite of the theory of the price of production, his law of value governed actual exchange relations, because it regulated the movement of prices on the one side, and on the other the prices of production themselves?

In short, if there is any rational meaning in the tissue of logical arguments on which Marx founds his theory of labour value I do not believe he taught or could have taught it in the less pretentious sense which Sombart now endeavours to attribute to it. For the rest, it is a matter which Sombart may himself settle with the followers of Marx. For those who, like myself, consider the Marxian theory of value a failure, it is of no importance whatever. For either Marx has maintained his law of value in the more pretentious sense that it corresponds with reality, and if so we agree with Sombart's view that, maintained in this sense, it is false; or he did not ascribe any real authority to it, and then, in my opinion, it cannot be construed in any sense whatever which would give it the smallest scientific importance. It is practically and theoretically a nullity.

It is true that about this Sombart is of a very different opinion. I willingly accept an express invitation from this able and learned man (who expects much for the progress of science from a keen and kindly encounter of opinions) to reconsider the "criticism of Marx" on the ground of his new interpretation. I am also quite pleased to settle this particular point with him. I do so with the full consciousness that I am no longer dealing with a "criticism of Marx," such as Sombart invited me to revise on the strength of his new interpretation, but am dispensing purely a "criticism of Sombart."

What, then, according to Sombart, does the existence of value as a "fact of thought" mean? It means that the "idea of value is an aid to our thought which we employ in order to make the phenomena of economic life comprehensible." More exactly, the function of the idea of value is " to cause to pass before us, defined by quantity, the commodities which, as goods for use, are different in quality. It is clear that I fulfil this postulate if I imagine cheese, silk, and blacking as nothing but products of human labour in the abstract. and only relate them to each other quantitatively as quantities of labour, the amount of the quantity being determined by a third factor, common to all and measured by units of time". [9]

So far all goes well, till we come to a certain little hitch. For certainly it is admissible in itself for some scientific purposes, to abstract from all sorts of differences, which things may exhibit in one way or another, and to consider in them only one property, which is common to them all, and which, as a common property, furnishes the ground for comparison, commensurability, &c. In this very way mechanical dynamics, for instance, for the purpose of many of its problems rightly abstracts altogether from the form, colour, density, and structure of bodies in motion, and regards them only as masses; propelled billiard-balls, flying cannonballs, running children, trains in motion, falling stones, and moving planets, are looked upon simply as moving bodies. It is not less admissible or less to the purpose to conceive cheese, silk, blacking, as "nothing but products of human labour in the abstract."

The hitch begins when Sombart, like Marx, claims for *this* idea the name of the idea of value. This step of his–to go closely into the matter–admits conceivably of two constructions. The word "value," as we know it, in its double application to value in use and value in exchange, is already used in scientific as well as in ordinary language to denote definite phenomena. Sombart's nomenclature, therefore, involves the claim either that property of things, i.e., the being a product of labour, which is alone taken into consideration, is the deciding factor for all cases of value in the ordinary scientific sense, and thus represents, for example, the phenomena of exchange value; or, without any arrière pensée of this kind, his nomenclature may be a purely arbitrary one; and, unfortunately for nomenclatures of that kind, there is as guide no fixed compulsory law, but only good judgment and a sense of fitness.

If we take the second of the two constructions, if the application of the term "value" to "embodied labour" does not carry with it the claim that embodied labour is the substance of exchange value, then the matter would be very harmless. It would be only a perfectly admissible abstraction, connected, it is true, with a most unpractical, inappropriate, and misleading nomenclature. It would be as if it suddenly occurred to a natural philosopher to give to the different bodies which, by abstraction of form, colour, structure, &c., he had conceived of solely as masses, the name of "active forces," a term which we know has already established rights, denoting a function of mass and velocity, that is to say, something very different from mere mass. There would be no scientific error in this, however, only a (practically very dangerous) gross inappropriateness of nomenclature.

But our case is obviously different. It is different with Marx and different with Sombart. And here, therefore, the hitch assumes larger proportions.

My esteemed opponent will certainly admit that we cannot make any abstraction we like to suit any scientific purpose we like. For instance, to start by conceiving the different bodies as "nothing but masses," which is legitimate in certain dynamic problems, would be plainly inadmissible in regard to acoustic or optical problems. Even within dynamics it is certainly inadmissible to abstract from shape and consistency, when setting forth, for instance, the law of wedges. These examples prove that even in science "thoughts" and "logic" cannot go quite away from facts. For science, too, the saying holds good, *"Est modus in rebus, sunt certi denique fines."* And I think that I may show, without danger of a contradiction from my esteemed opponent, that those "definite limits" consist in this, that in all cases only those peculiarities may be disregarded which are irrelevant to the phenomenon under investigation–N.B., *really, actually* irrelevant. On the other hand, one must leave to the remainder–to the skeleton, as it were–of the conception which is to be subjected to further study everything that is actually relevant on the concrete side. Let us apply this to our own case.

The Marxian teaching in a very emphatic way bases the scientific investigation and criticism of the *exchange relations of commodities* on the conception of commodities as "nothing but products." Sombart endorses this, and in certain rather indefinite· statements–which, on account of their indefiniteness, I do not discuss with him–he even goes so far as to view the foundations of the whole economic existence of man in the light of that abstraction. [10]

That embodied labour alone is of importance in the first (exchange), or even in the second case (economic existence), Sombart himself does not venture to affirm. He contents himself by asserting that with that conception the "fact *most important* economically and objectively" is brought into prominence. [11] I will not dispute this statement, only it must certainly not be taken to mean that all the other important facts besides labour are so completely subordinate that they might be almost, if not altogether disregarded, from their insignificance. Nothing could be less true. It is in the highest degree important for the economic existence of human beings whether, for instance, the land which they inhabit is like the valley of the Rhone, or the desert of Sahara, or Greenland; and it is also a matter of great importance whether human labour is aided by a previously accumulated stock of goods– a factor which also cannot be referred exclusively to labour. Labour is certainly *not* the objectively most important circumstance for many goods, especially as regards exchange relations. We may mention, as instances, trunks of old oak trees, beds of coal, and plots of land; and even if it be admitted that it is so for the greater part of commodities, still the fact must be emphasised that the influence of the other factors, which are determining factors beside labour, is so important that actual exchange relations diverge considerably from the line which would correspond with the embodied labour by itself.

But if work is not the sole important factor in exchange relations and exchange value, but only *one,* even though the most powerful, important factor among others–a *primus inter pares,* as it were–then, according to what has been already said, it is simply incorrect and inadmissible to base upon labour alone a conception of value which is synonymous with exchange value; it is just as wrong and inadmissible as if a natural philosopher were to base the "active force" on the mass of the bodies alone, and were by abstraction to eliminate velocity from his calculation.

I am truly astonished that Sombart did not see or feel this, and all the more so because in formulating his opinions he incidentally made use of expressions the incongruity of which, with his own premises, is so striking that one would have thought he could not fail to be struck by it. His starting-point is that the character of commodities, as products of social labour, represents the economically and objectively most important feature in them, and he proves it by saying that the supply to mankind of economic goods, *"natural conditions being equal,"* is *in the main* dependent on the development of the social productive power of labour, and thence he draws the conclusion that this feature finds its adequate economic expression in the conception of value which rests upon labour alone. This thought he twice repeats on pages 576 and 577 in Somewhat different terms, but the expression "adequate" recurs each time unchanged.

Now, I ask, is it not on the contrary evident that the conception of value as grounded upon labour alone is *not* adequate to the premise that labour is merely the most important among several important facts, but goes far beyond it. It would have been adequate only if the premise had affirmed that labour is the only important fact. But this Sombart by no means asserted. He maintains that the significance of labour is very great in regard to exchange relations and for human life generally, greater than the significance of any other factor; and for such a condition of things the Marxian formula of value, according to which labour alone is all-important, is an expression as little adequate as it would be to put down $1 + 1/2 + 1/4$ as equal to 1 only.

Not only is the assertion of the "adequate" conception of value not apposite, but it seems to me that there lurks behind it a little touch of wiliness–quite unintended by Sombart. While expressly admitting that the Marxian value does *not* stand the test of facts, Sombart demanded an asylum for the " outlawed" value in the thought of the theoretic economist. From this asylum, however, he unexpectedly makes a clever sally into the concrete world when he again maintains that his conception of value is adequate to the objectively most relevant fact, or in more pretentious words–that *"a technical fact which objectively governs* the economic existence of human society has found in it its adequate economic expression" (p. 577).

I think one may justly protest against such a proceeding. It is a case of one thing or the other. Either the Marxian value claims to be in harmony with actual facts, in which case it should come out boldly with this assertion and not seek to escape the thorough test of facts by entrenching itself behind the position that it had not meant to affirm any actual fact but only to construct "an aid for our thought"; or else it does seek to protect itself behind this rampart, it does avoid the thorough test of fact, and in that case it ought not to claim by the indirect means of vague assertions a kind of concrete significance which could justly belong to it only if it had stood that testing by facts which it had distinctly avoided. The phrase "the adequate expression of the *ruling fact*" signifies nothing less than that Marx is *in the main* even *empirically right.* Well and good. If Sombart or any one else wishes to affirm that let him do so openly. Let him leave off playing with the mere "fact of thought" and put the matter plainly to the test of actual fact. This test would show what the difference is between the complete facts and the "adequate expression of the ruling fact." Until then, however, I may content myself with asserting that in regard to Sombart's views we have not to deal with a harmless variation of a permissible but merely inappropriately named abstraction, but with a pretentious incursion into the domain of the actual, for which all justification by evidence is omitted and even evaded.

There is another inadmissibly pretentious assertion of Marx's which I think Sombart has accepted without sufficient criticism; the statement, namely, that it is only by conceiving commodities as "nothing but products" of social labour that it becomes possible to our thought to bring them into quantitative relation with each other–to make them "commensurable," and, therefore, "to render" the phenomena of the economic world "accessible" to our thought. [12] Would Sombart have found it possible to accept this assertion if he had subjected it to criticism? Could he really have thought that it is only by means of the Marxian idea of value that exchange relations are made accessible to scientific thought, or not at all? I cannot believe it. Marx's well-known dialectical argument on page 12 of the first volume can have had no convincing power for a Sombart. Sombart sees and knows as well as I do that not only products of labour, but pure products of nature too, are put into quantitative relation in exchange, and are therefore practically commensurable with each other as well as with the products of labour. And yet, according to him, we cannot conceive of them as commensurable except by reference to an attribute which they do trot possess, and which, though it can be ascribed to products of labour as far as quality is concerned, cannot be imputed to them in regard to quantity since, as has been admitted, products of labour too do not exchange in proportion to the labour embodied in them. Should not that rather be a sign to the unbased theorist that, in spite of Marx, the true common denominator–the true common factor in exchange–has still to be sought for, and sought for in another direction than that taken by Marx?

This leads me to a last point on which I must touch in regard to Sombart. Sombart wishes to trace back the opposition which exists between the Marxian system on the one side, and the adverse theoretic systems–especially of the so-called Austrian economists–on the other, to a dispute about method. Marx, he says, represents an extreme objectivity. We others represent a subjectivity which runs into psychology. Marx does not trace out the motives which determine individual subjects as economic agents in their mode of action, but he seeks the objective factors, the "economic conditions," which are *independent* of the will, and, I may add, often also of the knowledge, of the individual. He seeks to discover "what goes on beyond the control of the individual by the power of relations which are independent of him." We, on the contrary, "try to explain the processes of economic life in the last resort by a reference to the mind of the economic subject," and "plant the laws of economic life on a psychological basis." [13]

That is certainly one of the many subtle and ingenious observations which are to be found in Sombart's writings; but in spite of its essential soundness it does not seem to me to meet the main point. It does not meet me in regard to the past by explaining the position taken up hitherto by the critics towards Marx, and therefore it does not meet it as regards the future, demanding, as it does, an entirely new era of Marxian criticism, which has still to begin, for which there is "as good as no preparatory work done," [14] and in regard to which it would be necessary to decide first of all what is to be its method. [15]

The state of things appears to me to be rather this. The difference pointed out by Sombart in the method of investigation certainly exists. But the "old" criticism of Marx did not, so far as I personally can judge, attack his choice of method, but his mistakes in the application of his chosen method. As I have no right to speak of other critics of Marx I must speak of myself. Personally, as regards the question of method, I am in the position taken up by the literary man in the story in regard to literature: he allowed every kind of literature with the exception of the "genre ennuyeux." I allow every kind of method so long as it is practised in such a way as to produce some good results. I have nothing whatever to say against the objective method. I believe that in the region of those phenomena which are concerned with human action it can be an aid to the attainment of real knowledge. That certain objective factors can enter into systematic connection with typical human actions, while those who are acting under the influence of the connection are not clearly conscious of it, I willingly admit, and I have myself drawn attention to such phenomena. For instance, when statistics prove that suicides are specially numerous in certain months, say July and November, or that the number of marriages rises and falls according as harvests are plentiful or the reverse, I am convinced that most of those who swell the contingent of suicides that occur in the months of July and November never realise that it is July and November; and also that the decision of those who are anxious to marry is not directly affected by the consideration that the means of subsistence are temporarily cheaper. [16] At the same time the discovery of such an objective connection is undoubtedly of scientific value.

At this juncture, however, I must make several reservations–self-evident reservations, I think. Firstly, it seems clear to me that the knowledge of such an objective connection, without the knowledge of the subjective links which help to form the chain of causation, is by no means the highest degree of knowledge, but that a full comprehension will only be attained by a knowledge of both the internal and external links of the chain. And so it seems to me that the obvious answer to Sombart's question ("whether the objective movement in the science of political economy is justified as exclusive, or as simply complementary?" [17]) is, that the objective movement can be justified only as complementary.

Secondly, I think, but as it is a matter of opinion, I do not wish to press the point with opponents, that it is just in the region of economics, where we have to deal so largely with conscious and calculated human action, that the first of the two sources of knowledge, the objective source, can at the best contribute a very poor and, especially when standing alone, an altogether inadequate part of the total of attainable knowledge.

Thirdly–and this concerns the criticism of Marx in particular–I must ask with all plainness that if any use is made of the objective method it should be the right use. If external objective connections are shown to exist, which, like fate, control action with or without the knowledge, with or without the will of the doer, let them be shown to exist in their correctness. And Marx has not done this. He has not proved his fundamental proposition that labour alone governs exchange relations either objectively, from the external, tangible, objective world of facts, with which on the contrary they are in opposition, or subjectively, from the motives of the exchanging parties; but he gives it to the world in the form of an abortive dialectic, more arbitrary and untrue to facts than has probably ever before been known in the history of our science.

And one thing more. Marx did not hold fast to the "objective" pale. He could not help referring to the motives of the operators as to an active force in his system. He does this pre-eminently by his appeal to " competition." Is it too much to demand that if he introduces subjective interpolation~ into his system they should be correct, well founded, and non-contradictory? And this reasonable demand Marx has continually contravened. It is because of these offences with which, I say again, the choice of method has nothing to do, but which are forbidden by the laws of every method, that I have opposed and do oppose the Marxian theory as a wrong theory. It represents, in my opinion, the one forbidden genre–the genre, wrong theories.

I am, and have long been, at the standpoint towards which Sombart seeks to direct the future criticism of Marx, which he thinks has still to be originated. He thinks "that a sympathetic study and criticism of the Marxian system ought to be attempted in the following way: Is the objective movement in the science of political economy justified as exclusive or as complementary? If an affirmative answer be given, then it may further be asked: Is the Marxian method of a quantitative measurement of the economic facts by means of the idea of value as an aid to thought demanded Z If so, is labour properly chosen as the substance of the idea of value? ... If it is, can the Marxian reasoning, the edifice of system erected on it, its conclusions, &c., be disputed?"

In my own mind I long ago answered the first question of method in favour of a justification of the objective method as "complementary." I was, and am, also equally certain that, to keep to Sombart's words, "a quantitative measurement of economic facts is afforded by an idea of value as an aid to thought." To the third question, however, the question whether it is right to select labour as the substance of this idea of value, I have long given a decidedly negative answer; and the further question, the question whether the Marxian reasoning, conclusions, &c., can be disputed, I answer as decidedly in the affirmative.

What will be the final judgment of the world? Of that I have no manner of doubt. The Marxian system has a past and a present, but no abiding future. Of all sorts of scientific systems those which, like the Marxian a hollow dialectic, are based on a hollow dialectic, most surely doomed. A clever dialectic may make a temporary impression on the human mind, but cannot make a lasting one. In the long run facts and the secure linking of causes and effects win the day. In the domain of natural science such a work as Marx's would even now be impossible. In the very young social sciences it was able to attain influence, great influence, and it will probably only lose it very slowly, and that because it has its most powerful support not in the convinced intellect of its disciples, but in their hearts, their wishes, and their desires. It can also subsist for a long time on the large capital of authority which it has gained over many people. In the prefatory remarks to this article I said that Marx had been very fortunate as an author, and it appears to me that a circumstance which has contributed not a little to this good fortune is the fact that the conclusion of his system has appeared ten years after his death, and almost thirty years after the appearance of his first volume. If the teaching and the definitions of the third volume had been presented to the world simultaneously with the first volume, there would have been few unbased readers, I think, who would not have felt the logic of the first volume to be somewhat doubtful. Now a belief in an authority which has been rooted for thirty years forms a bulwark against the incursions of critical knowledge–a bulwark that will surely but slowly be broken down.

But even when this will have happened Socialism will certainly not be overthrown with the Marxian system, – neither practical nor theoretic Socialism. As there was a Socialism before Marx, so there will be one after him. That there is vital force in Socialism is shown, in spite of all exaggerations, not only by the renewed vitality which economic theory has undeniably gained by the appearance of the theoretic Socialists, but also by the celebrated "drop of social oil" with which the measures of practical statesmanship are nowadays everywhere lubricated, and in many cases not to their disadvantage. What there is, then, of vital force in Socialism, I say, the wiser minds among its leaders will not fail in good time to try to connect with a scientific system more likely to live. They will try to replace the supports which have become rotten. What purification of fermenting ideas will result from this connection the future will show. We may hope perhaps that things will not always go round and round in the same circle, that some errors may be shaken off for ever, and that some knowledge will be added permanently to the store of positive attainment, no longer to be disputed even by party passion.

Marx, however, will maintain a permanent place in the history of the social sciences for the same reasons and with the same mixture of positive and negative merits as his prototype Hegel. Both of them were philosophical geniuses. Both of them, each in his own domain, had an enormous influence upon the thought and feeling of whole generations, one might almost say even upon the spirit of the age. The specific theoretical work of each was a most ingeniously conceived structure, built up by a magical power of combination, of numerous storeys of thought, held together by a marvellous mental grasp, but–a house of cards.

[1] See the already repeatedly mentioned article *Zur Kritik des okonomischen Systems von Karl Marx* in the *Archiv fur Sociale Gesetzgebung und Statistik,* vol. vii., part 4, pp. 555 seq.
[2] See above, pp. 98-101.
[3] Hugo Landé, *Neue Zeit,* xi. p. 59
[4] *Loc. cit.,* p. 575, then pp. 584 seq.
[5] For example, i. 25; Equivalent = Exchangeable. "It is only as a value that it (linen) can be brought into relation with the coat as possessing an equal value or exchangeability with it." ... "When the coat as a thing of value is placed on an equality with the linen, the work existing in the former is made equal to the work existing in the latter." See besides pp. 27, 31 (the proportion in which coats and linen are exchangeable depends on the degree of value of the coats), p. 35 (where Marx declares human work to be the "real element of equality" in the house and the beds which exchange with each other), pp. 39, 40, 41, 42, 43, 50, 51, 52, 53 (Analysis of the price of commodities [but still of actual prices only!] leads to the determining of the amount of value), p. 60 (exchange value is the social contrivance for expressing the labour expended on a thing), p. 80 ("the price is the money name for the work realised in a commodity"), p. 141 ("the same exchange value, that is, the same quantum of realised social work"), p. 174 ("According to the universal law of value, for example, 10 lbs. of yarn are an equivalent for 10 lbs. of cotton and a quarter of a spindle ... if the same working time is needed to produce both sides of this equation"), and repeatedly in the same sense.
[6] Ibid., p. 575.
[7] I. 52.
[8] For example, i. 14, note 9.
[9] *Zur Kritik der okonamischen System von Karl Marx,* p. 574.
[10] For example, pp. 576, 577.
[11] p. 576.

[12] Ibid., pp. 574, 582. Sombart has not asserted this in so many words in his own name, but he approves a statement of C. Schmidt to this effect, and of which he only corrects an unimportant detail (p. 574). He says, moreover, that Marx's doctrine of value "performs" just this "service " (p. 582), and at all events he refrains entirely from denying it.

[13] Ibid., pp. 591 seq.

[14] Ibid., p. 556.

[15] pp. 593 seq.

[16] Somehow or other indeed an influence proceeding from the objective factor, and having a symptomatic connection with it, must produce effects on the actors; for instance, in the examples given in the text, the effect on the nerves of the heat of July, or the depressing, melancholy autumn weather, may increase the tendency to suicide. Then the influence coming from the "objective factor" issues, as it were, in a more general typical stimulus, such as derangement of the nerves or melancholy, and in this way affects action. I maintain firmly (in opposition to Sombart's observation, p. 593), that conformity to law in outward action is not to be expected without conformity to law in inward stimulus; but at the same time (and this will perhaps satisfy Sombart from the standpoint of his own method) I hold it to be quite possible that we can observe objective conformities to law in human action, and fix them inductively without knowing and understanding their origin in inward stimulus. Therefore there is no law-determined action without law-determined stimulus, but yet there is law-determined action without knowledge of the stimulus of it.

[17] Ibid., p. 593.

www.ingramcontent.com/pod-product-compliance
Lightning Source LLC
Chambersburg PA
CBHW022128280326
41933CB00007B/592